FEEDBACK
Fitness

Three Simple Steps for leaders to have Courageous Conversations that drive performance

Sue Anderson

Published by Good2gr8 Coaching
PO Box 148
Buninyong VIC 3357
Australia

Copyright © 2024 Sue Anderson
First published 2024

All rights reserved. No part of this publication may be reproduced, stored in a retrieval system, or transmitted in any form or by any means whatsoever without prior permission of the copyright owner. Apply in writing to the publisher.

Edited by Scharlaine Cairns, Charlie C. Editorial Pty Ltd
Designed by Di Zign Pty Ltd
Cover design by Di Zign Pty Ltd,
   adapted from an original idea by Maria Oriola
Back cover image: Melissa Decarli
Typeset in Heuristica 10pt and Helvetica Neue
Printed in Australia

ISBN: 978-0-9875609-1-9 (Paperback)
ISBN: 978-0-9875609-2-6 (e-Book)

 A catalogue record for this book is available from the National Library of Australia

Disclaimer:
The names and identifying details in this book have been changed to protect the privacy of individuals.

The URLs in this book were current at the time of publication. The author and publisher are unable to guarantee the ongoing currency of any URLs appearing in this book.

Contents

Acknowledgements	viii
Introduction	ix
Leaders' reluctance to offer feedback	x
Problems caused by not being Feedback Fit	x
The language used in this book	xi
Chapter 1: The Future of Feedback	**1**
Employee recruitment and retention: A key challenge	1
Clarifying expectations in multigenerational workplaces	2
Navigating the shift to remote and hybrid work	2
Addressing employee engagement challenges	2
The evolving landscape of feedback: Listening skills for leaders	3
Building trust through feedback	4
Increased emphasis on psychological safety in the workplace	4
A certainty: The need to navigate courageous feedback conversations	5
Chapter 2: What's Really Going On	**7**
What is really going on in your feedback conversations?	7
Chapter 3: Feedback Fitness Framework	**21**
Overview of the Feedback Fitness framework	21
Chapter 4: Introduction to the Warm-up Conversation	**27**
The importance of a full warm-up conversation *before* offering feedback	27
Types of warm-up conversations	28
The warm-up process	31
Chapter 5: Feedback Self-assessments	**33**
Make friends with offering feedback	33
The Feedback Offering self-assessment	36
Make friends with receiving feedback	42
The Feedback Receiving self-assessment	46

Contents

Chapter 6: Three Feedback TIPs — 53
    Tailored, Intention and Permission — 53
    Making it fun — 63

Chapter 7: Introduction to the Workout Conversation — 75
    The workout conversation — 76

Chapter 8: Acknowledgement Feedback — 83
    What is acknowledgement feedback? — 83

Chapter 9: Evaluation Feedback — 87
    The purpose of evaluation feedback — 87
    How to offer evaluation feedback — 88
    Keep your 'but' out of your feedback conversations! — 90
    What if the recipient feels upset? — 91

Chapter 10: Guidance Feedback — 93
    What is guidance feedback? — 93
    What is the purpose of guidance feedback? — 94
    How to offer guidance feedback — 94

Chapter 11: The Three Types of Feedback — 97
    Make friends with evaluation feedback — 99
    Offering feedback online: 'Yes' or 'No'? — 102

Chapter 12: The Cool-down Conversations — 107
    The purpose of cool-down conversations — 107

Chapter 13: Receiving Feedback — 117
    The Feedback Receiving formula — 117
    The Feedback Receiving self-assessment — 118

Chapter 14: Mindset — 125
    Beliefs about feedback — 125
    Thinking styles — 126

Chapter 15: Power — 137
   The power to choose what we BELIEVE — 138
   What are beliefs? — 140
   The power to choose how we FEEL — 142
   The power to choose what we SAY — 148
   The power to choose what we DO — 149

Chapter 16: Confidence and Esteem — 157
   An overview — 157
   Strategy 1: Consider confidence and esteem as two different things — 157
   Strategy 2: Confidence is contextual — 158
   Strategy 3: 'Esteem' is a *vurrrrb* [verb]! — 159
   Strategy 4: Feedback is about performance/behaviour, not your worth as a person — 161
   Strategy 5: Flat line esteem—esteem does not go up and down — 162
   Strategy 6: Feedback is useful, but you don't *need* it to feel good about yourself — 163

Chapter 17: Conclusion — 165
Endnotes — 167
Work with Sue — 171
By the same author — 172

Acknowledgements

I wish to acknowledge all the wonderful people who, in their own unique ways, contributed to the creation of this book:

- Chris Cartledge
- Cleo Anderson
- Jarvis Cartledge
- Jazmyn Cartledge
- Jane Bedggood
- Jane Anderson
- Donna McGeorge
- Alison Crabb
- Ros Weadman
- Maria Orilola
- Zoe Routh
- Dr Libby Brook
- Scharlaine Cairns
- Diana Murray

I extend my thanks to them all.

Sue Anderson

Introduction

I've got some feedback for you.

This sentence has the power to send you into a frenzy of anticipatory dread and anxiety. Even if you are unsure what the feedback is about, your brain may scramble to come up with something you *must* have done wrong. Your old friend 'Not good enough' shows up, armed with a myriad of examples of where you have failed. Your heart starts to race, your armpits sweat, and your mouth starts drying out.

But then:

The CEO really sang your praises in our senior executive meeting this morning. She wants to catch up with you, herself, to thank you for the way you handled the Jones case. She was really impressed.

Sweet relief! You feel the tension leaving your body. You are exhilarated!

How can two simple sentences, like 'I've got some feedback for you' and 'She was really impressed', have two completely different effects on your emotions?

This book is intended to explore why the initial reaction to 'feedback' might be one of fear and dread, and how that also provides an opportunity to grow and learn. Strategies and solutions will be explored in regard to how to think and feel differently about both the offering and the receiving of feedback.

Receiving feedback is one thing but, if you feel a bit weird and awkward about offering feedback, you are not alone. I have spent more than ten years having confidential conversations **about** feedback with leaders in the workplace. I have listened to their beliefs, emotions, fears and struggles relating to feedback conversations. Those leaders have shared their innermost fears, their struggles and their triumphs relating to feedback they have offered and received. When it comes to describing their own feedback conversations, they have often use words such as 'difficult', 'challenging', 'nervous' and 'dread', before they have moved on to other words like 'courage', 'confidence', and 'inspired'.

It is through these conversations about feedback that I have been able to create my Feedback Fitness framework. In the process I have also looked at other frameworks and research related to feedback. I have coached individual leaders to implement the framework and have delivered my Feedback Fitness workshop hundreds of times across a variety of industries. My framework provides a structure and process which enables leaders to have confident and courageous feedback conversations. The process reduces friction and frustration and improves the effectiveness of future feedback conversations for both the person offering the feedback and the person receiving it.

Conversations of the Feedback Fitness kind are missing from most professional relationships. You will be amazed by what you can learn about yourself and others when you listen deeply to those others during your feedback conversations.

The Feedback Fitness framework sheds light on blind spots for both the person offering the feedback and the person receiving it and invites those involved to think about feedback in a way they never have before.

Leaders' reluctance to offer feedback

Common fears that leaders have about offering feedback include:
- What if people become upset, angry or withdrawn?
- What if I damage our relationship and it becomes awkward?
- What if they make a complaint about me?
- What if they accuse me of bullying them?
- What if they leave? Our team can't afford to lose another member at this busy time.

Problems caused by not being Feedback Fit

Feedback drives performance. If the Feedback Fitness in your team is low, and you are not part of an organisation that supports a Feedback Fit culture, problems like the following can arise.

- You don't have conversations that it would be useful to have.
- People stop offering feedback (adopting a position of: 'Let them figure it out for themselves').
- You have a 'nice and polite' culture, but miss identifying and rectifying real issues.
- You miss opportunities to improve.
- Lost productivity—meaning it's expensive!

The language used in this book

The following provides explanations of the important language choices made in this book.

'Offering' feedback, rather than 'giving' feedback

Throughout this book, you will notice the use of the term '*offering* feedback', rather than '*giving* feedback'. This is a deliberate choice.

If I 'give' someone feedback, it sounds like they have no choice other than to accept it. When I 'offer' them feedback, they can decide:

- whether they are open to considering it
- how they will think about the feedback
- whether they will take what is said on board or not.

> **Tip:**
> I prefer the 'offering' option because it implies choice. That's more empowering!

The 'other person', rather than the 'team member' or 'direct report'

This book is aimed at people in leadership roles. Because of that, I was very tempted to use the word 'leader' to describe the person offering the feedback and the terms 'team member' or 'direct report' to describe the person being offered it. I chose not to do that because, ideally, both parties in the relationship offer and receive feedback from each other at different times.

You will sometimes see the (at times awkward) use of 'the other person' for describing the recipient of feedback. This reference is to the person in the feedback conversation to whom feedback is being offered, but from whom feedback is possibly also being received.

> **Tip:**
> Think of feedback occurring in a series of two-way conversations, rather than as part of a one-off, one-way, event.

'Useful' feedback, rather than 'positive' or 'negative' feedback'

Let's keep it real! Many people are not skilled in offering feedback.

Suppose you are offered poorly delivered feedback by someone you can't stand. You may feel irritated, annoyed or frustrated. You could label that particular feedback experience as 'negative'. But let's suppose you were open to the person's feedback, considered it, then implemented it, and the impact of that was immediate and fabulous. You then feel wonderful!

Do we then label that feedback as 'positive' or 'negative'? It is neither—so let's go with a more neutral description: The feedback was 'useful'.

Alternatively, you could be offered the most eloquently expressed and beautifully delivered feedback from someone with whom you have a great relationship. You might feel 'positive' in the moment, but the feedback might not be useful. You can't action it and the person who delivered it hasn't considered the bigger context—so you feel frustrated. Do you label that feedback as 'positive' or 'negative?' It is neither—so let's go with a more neutral description: The feedback was 'not useful'.

Resist judging the feedback as positive or negative, and stick with terms for describing it that are similar to 'useful' or 'not useful'; 'actionable' or 'not actionable'; and 'effective' or 'ineffective'.

Introduction

> **Tip:**
> Keep in mind, it is the person receiving the feedback who decides whether the feedback you offer is useful or not. We often mistakenly believe the feedback we are offering is fabulous!

'Word on the Street'

Over the past two years I have surveyed and interviewed hundreds of people in preparation for this book.

When you see a heading like the one above, containing the words 'Word on the Street', the content which follows it is the result of my own research. I have left the data as raw as possible (except for correcting a few typos and reducing the repetition of responses), so you can gain insight into the current thinking that is 'out there' in the real world.

Okay, let's begin!

1
The Future of Feedback

As we navigate the evolving landscapes of workplaces worldwide, it is clear that a fresh and innovative approach to feedback is needed. We are all aware that workplaces are constantly changing, necessitating a shift in how we engage in future feedback conversations. Let's look at some trends shaping the workplace landscape of 2024 and beyond.

Employee recruitment and retention: A key challenge

Have you recently struggled to fill vacancies in your team? If you have, you are not alone. Many leaders are finding it increasingly difficult to recruit good team members and keep them.[1] You can use feedback conversations as part of the interview process and, also, to keep your team members engaged by linking feedback to progress towards goals that are meaningful to them. 'Employee engagement is an essential part of employee retention.'[2]

Studies show that 'employees who perceive purpose and significance in their work are three times more likely to stay with their companies'.[3] Understanding the importance of their work fosters the employees' sense of investment, leading to higher retention rates.

Feedback can be used to demonstrate your respect for each team member. Taking the time to offer thoughtful, meaningful feedback shows that you are respectful of a team member and support the individual's development in the role. Research indicates employees who feel respected are 110% more likely to stay in their jobs.[4]

> **Tip:**
> The future of feedback will involve utilising feedback conversations to help recruit team members and to allow team members to see they are making progress in meaningful work.

Clarifying expectations in multigenerational workplaces

Hopefully your team is made up of a delicious mix of individuals, making a unique melting pot of work and communication styles. For the first time in history, we have five generations working together.[5] This kind of diversity within your team brings a unique blend of work and communication styles, resulting in both benefits and challenges. While advantage does lie in a diversity of ideas and perspectives, challenges also arise from differing expectations regarding communication, leadership, teamwork and feedback.

> **Tip:**
> The future of feedback will involve clarifying expectations about feedback with every member of the team, while respecting their differences.

Navigating the shift to remote and hybrid work

As you may have experienced in your organisation, the traditional workplace has undergone a transformative shift, with a substantial portion of the workforce operating remotely or in hybrid arrangements.[6] Many leaders continue to find it difficult to arrange face-to-face meetings, with online interactions becoming the norm. Rather than not offering feedback, or delaying it until the next time both you and an employee are in the office together, you may need to offer feedback online or over the phone, rather than face-to-face.

> **Tip:**
> The future of feedback will involve adapting to remote and hybrid work scenarios by leveraging various communication methods for feedback, including in-person, online, and by phone.

Addressing employee engagement challenges

In 2024, employee engagement remains a persistent challenge for leaders globally, with a significant percentage of employees disengaged at work.[7] Recognising the importance of feedback in this context is crucial, because a lack of feedback contributes to increased disengagement. It is essential that you offer regular feedback to encourage the growth and development of team members, because this helps to keep them engaged.

> **Tip:**
> The future of feedback will involve using feedback conversations to drive engagement by encouraging growth and development in your team members.

The evolving landscape of feedback: Listening skills for leaders

In a changing work environment, feedback mechanisms are also evolving. A global study of 3875 employees (by Zenger Folkman)[8] highlighted the importance of leaders' abilities to listen when providing effective feedback. Leaders who carefully listen to employees' perspectives *before* offering feedback have been rated as providing the most honest, useful and effective feedback. This emphasises the need for leaders to develop advanced listening skills as more employees demand leaders who actively engage in the feedback process.

I found the Zenger Folkman research fascinating! The research found the ability of leaders to provide effective feedback was closely tied to their capacity to *listen*. The feedback we offer will be more effective if we listen *before* we offer it. Listening is intricately linked to communication and trust, which further emphasises its importance in feedback conversations.

The research indicates leaders who found it hard to listen, and who offered advice *before* asking the team members' perspective, were rated poorly as feedback givers.[9]

> **Tip:**
> The future of feedback will involve leaders developing advanced listening skills to enhance the quality and impact of the feedback they offer.

Building trust through feedback

Trust between leaders and team members is a cornerstone of effective leadership and employee engagement. Building and maintaining trust requires leaders to embody such qualities as empathy, openness, transparency, fairness, consideration of the opinions of others, and the ability to handle tough conversations. Ensuring that feedback conversations take place in a psychologically safe manner is a powerful tool for building and reinforcing trust within an organisation.

> **Tip:**
> The future of feedback will involve using feedback as a means to build and strengthen trust between leaders and team members.

Increased emphasis on psychological safety in the workplace

Leaders need to navigate the delicate balance between psychological safety, providing feedback, and holding team members to account.[10] This is especially important when the feedback is evaluative in nature—particularly when the recipient of the feedback is not meeting expectations. Professor Amy Edmondson, a world leading authority on psychological safety and the Novartis Professor of Leadership and Management at the Harvard Business School, emphasises the importance of teaching behaviours associated with psychological safety. She believes creating a safe team culture for feedback conversations is crucial and says that:

> *Giving and receiving feedback happens best in a psychologically safe environment.*[11]

··· What Dr Libby Brook says ···

Libby Brook is an organisational psychologist and expert in psychological health and safety. She has said the following on the topic:

> *Psychological health and safety is really about reducing the risk to people's psychological health and creating an*

> *environment where people feel healthy and able to work to their best, get satisfaction from work and all the good things that people want, like achievement and growth. I think there's a fear about hurting people, which may be exacerbated by a fear of the feedback conversation causing psychological injury.*[12]

> **Tip:**
> The future of feedback will involve an increased focus on providing feedback in a psychologically safe manner.

A certainty: The need to navigate courageous feedback conversations

I've researched the work of several workplace futurists who have predicted the qualities leaders will need in 2024 and beyond. Common trends indicate leaders will need to be (even) more emotionally intelligent, humble, inclusive, vulnerable, and empowered. Some futurists predict leaders will need to excel at empathy, be excellent at communicating and be skilful at decision-making. Leaders need to be visionary, flexible, authentic, courageous and collaborative. The list sounds exhausting!

While it can be useful to make predictions, only one thing is guaranteed—there will be tough conversations; and I'm 100% certain that a high number of those tough conversations will involve feedback. While it's important to develop the skills required to have tough feedback conversations, it is also necessary to create a culture in your team and within your organisation in which feedback conversations are approached with confidence and courage.

> ··· What Simon Sinek says ···
>
> Speaker and best-selling author Simon Sinek has said the following about feedback conversations:
>
> *Some of the human skills that are underappreciated and undertrained in this day and age are: how to have difficult*

> *conversations, how to have an effective confrontation, and how to give and receive feedback.*[13]

> **Tip:**
> The future of feedback will involve having increased skills and courage to engage in tough conversations.

⋯ What Zoë Routh says ⋯

To gain further insights into the future of feedback, I interviewed leadership futurist Zoë Routh.[14] She outlined the following points.

- **Intent is key:** Leaders must be clear about the intent behind their feedback—and clear about it being constructive or positive. The purpose should focus on helping individuals grow into better leaders.
- **The three Cs of leadership:** Future leadership requires a focus on **c**reativity, **c**ollaboration and **c**ompassion. Compassion in feedback needs to be especially emphasised, given the potential for increased volatility and uncertainty in the future.
- **Inclusion and belonging:** Creating a sense of place and community is crucial for psychological safety and effective feedback. Leaders must work on fostering inclusion and belonging, to provide a foundation for constructive feedback.

According to Routh:

> *The future of feedback involves leaders embracing the three Cs—creativity, collaboration and compassion—and cultivating a sense of inclusion and belonging within their teams.*

Are you ready to embrace the future of feedback? In the remainder of this book, we will be exploring strategies and skills to prepare you for the evolving dynamics of workplace communication and leadership.

Let's prepare you for the future of feedback, now.

2
What's Really Going On

Clear is kind. Unclear is unkind. Sometimes speaking the truth feels like we are being unkind, especially when sharing difficult information or feedback. But in reality, dancing around the truth is unkind. When we avoid stating the truth when we are vague or ambiguous under the guise of being kind—it is often because we are trying to lessen the discomfort for ourselves, not for the other person.

Dr Brené Brown[15]

What is really going on in your feedback conversations?

What is the quality of your relationship with feedback? Are you casually dating, or are you deeply committed? On the following pages are several factors I've identified as characteristic of feedback conversations in the workplace. You might be experiencing some, or even all, of them.

Beliefs about feedback interfere with our feedback conversations

What you believe about feedback holds your feedback behaviour in place. What immediately comes to mind for you when you hear the word 'feedback'? Your childhood experiences, and feedback from family, teachers, coaches and your peers all impact your current thinking about feedback. Think back to your first job, what was your very first workplace experience of feedback?

Useful beliefs about feedback
- Feedback helps me grow and learn in my role.
- I'd rather know now, rather than in three months.
- I can choose how I respond to the feedback offered to me.

Limiting beliefs about feedback
- Feedback means I've done something wrong.
- Feedback means I'm not good enough.
- Feedback makes me feel uncomfortable.

You can complete all the feedback skills training in the world but, if you continue to believe that feedback conversations are a threat and are dangerous, you will avoid participating in those conversations. That does make sense when we consider that we are always trying to keep ourselves safe; including psychologically safe.

If we believe feedback is about improving, learning and exploring our potential, we will be more comfortable with struggle, making mistakes and accepting the role of learner. We will be more open to considering feedback. We will value feedback and appreciate it when it is offered. We might even ask for it! (In Chapter 15, 'Power', we will explore how to develop more useful beliefs about feedback.)

▶▶ One person's story: Anna

Anna, one of the leaders I have coached, expressed the following to me:

> I had been in a leadership role for two years. I'd already attended a 'How to have Courageous Conversations' workshop—but I was still avoiding having them. I felt like an imposter. My limiting belief was, 'Leaders SHOULD know how to have these conversations—I don't, so I'm not a good leader.' I started to wonder if I was leadership material.
>
> The main reason I was afraid to have feedback conversations was . . . a risk of high conflict. And, consequently, without my peers and line manager knowing, I often buried my head in the sand and avoided the conversations, hoping things would magically improve on their own. Of course, they didn't.

> *I felt ashamed and guilty because I wasn't addressing the issues and having the hard conversations. I was already trying to step into my power—and I could be courageous at certain times, but I was also a people-pleaser and I didn't take feedback well (although I pretended to). I was good at supporting people and that's how I tried to deal with it; I just tried to give them more support. I thought, 'Maybe if I try hard enough, they will change.' Again, this was wishful thinking on my part.*
>
> *I wasn't addressing the fundamental things like dynamics within the team and behaviour that wasn't aligned with our values. I didn't feel I could ask for help. I'd never admit to, and be vulnerable about, my lack of confidence in having these conversations. I didn't know how to deal with it. There was no Brené Brown podcast to listen to back then!'*

I have included Anna's story here because it is one to which many leaders can relate. Until Anna develops more useful beliefs about feedback, it is going to be hard for her to build her confidence. If you can relate to that, you are not alone.

This book offers you a process and practical tools you can use to build your confidence when it comes to having feedback conversations.

Fear of emotions impacts our feedback conversations

Often, we are not fearful of the feedback, but it's the emotions we experience before, during and after feedback conversations that we are trying to avoid. We are apprehensive about feedback conversations because we are afraid of how the feedback might make us (or the other person) feel.

When people fear feedback conversations, it's often because they believe the feedback has the power to 'make them feel something'.

Following is a list of common examples of how people don't want to feel (or want the other person to feel) in feedback conversations:
- uncomfortable
- embarrassed

- awkward
- fearful
- overwhelmed
- like a failure
- useless
- ashamed
- worried
- stupid
- not good enough
- anxious
- guilty
- humiliated

Many people try to control the emotions they feel in feedback conversations. If people have limiting beliefs about feedback, they can experience anxiety and dread in the lead up to a feedback conversation (even when they don't know what the conversation will be about)! You may have experienced these feelings, followed by sweet relief when the other person starts the conversation with the reassuring words, 'I just wanted to pass on some great feedback from the CEO about your work.'

I was delivering a Feedback Fitness workshop and one participant shared that she would never tell anyone if she was great at receiving feedback. Curious, I asked what she meant. Her response was: 'If I said I'm great at receiving feedback and open to it, people will give me lots of direct feedback, and I'm worried how that will make me feel.'

It wasn't the feedback she was worried about; it was how the feedback would **make her feel**. Her language gave a clue that she believes feedback can make her feel something she does not want to feel. (In Chapter 15, 'Power', we will explore how you can have more choice regarding how you feel.)

Protective 'armour' prevents the feedback conversations being heard

Often, it's not the feedback that's the problem; it's the 'armour' we use to protect ourselves from the emotions that get in the way of the feedback conversation. When we are fearful of feedback and 'how it will make us feel', we armour up—trying to protect ourselves. But the armour is heavy and stops us from listening.

American researcher, Dr Brené Brown, refers to it as our 'armour of self-protection':

> *We all use armor to protect ourselves, but that armor is heavy and prevents us from growing, being seen and being in connection with others.*[16]

Here are examples of 'armours' you might observe in yourself and others before, during and after feedback conversations:

- perfectionism
- sarcasm
- defensiveness
- avoidance.

Suppose you lead a team of three people: David, Sam and Chevaan. You offer them feedback in your fortnightly one-on-one meetings. Their reactions to that feedback are as follows:

- David becomes emotional and offers to resign. He says he is a failure and starts getting tearful.
- Sam challenges, questions and argues with every statement you make. She says it's Chevaan who is holding up her work. She starts criticising your feedback-offering skills and tells you, 'You aren't a very good leader.'
- Chevaan stares blankly at you and offers one-word responses to your questions. He calls in sick the following day.

David, Sam and Chevaan have all displayed signs of different armours of self-protection. These are the types of responses dreaded by many people who offer feedback, and that dread is one of the reasons they are reluctant to even offer feedback. (We will explore the kind of self-protective armour just referred to in Chapter 15, 'Power'.)

Trying to be 'perfect' in our feedback conversations

If you are aiming for perfection in your feedback conversations—good luck! Feedback conversations are often messy and imperfect. Your armour gets in the way! Emotions complicate things. Feedback conversations involve humans trying to communicate while experiencing human emotions and they occur within a variety of complex contexts and degrees of relationships.

Think of Feedback Fit conversations as a series of ongoing conversations in which, ideally, both parties have discussed and agreed on the process beforehand. Feedback is not a speech, or something for which you write a script or rehearse and have only one chance at delivering perfectly. There is no perfect script.

Waiting for the perfect time, for you and the other person to be in the perfect mood, and then trying to say the perfect thing to gain the perfect response will result in procrastination—or worse, avoidance.

Be kind to yourself when it comes to feedback conversations. Most feedback conversations, especially challenging ones, occur in private. Therefore, it is highly likely you have not observed many skills for having challenging feedback conversations (unless you were the recipient of the feedback and, in that case, you were probably not observing the framework used by the person offering that feedback)!

When your self-talk about offering feedback is not useful (for example, Don't stuff it up! This is my one chance to get this feedback right. It must not go badly!'), it is normal to experience fear if you perceive offering feedback to be dangerous. This type of thinking takes you into 'all-or-nothing thinking': 'If I can't offer this feedback perfectly, I won't offer it at all.'

Worrying about feedback damaging relationships

I work as a consultant and, many years ago, I was asked by an organisation to come and present feedback (originating from a third party) to a team, because their performance was not meeting expectations. The CEO of the organisation, who had engaged me, explained that the relationship between the team and the manager had broken down, and he (the CEO) was 'unavailable' to deliver the feedback himself. As much as many leaders might like to, we can't always outsource tricky feedback conversations!

I understood this CEO's reasoning. It was much easier for me, as an outsider to come in and meet with the team and present the feedback to them. It wasn't *my* feedback. I didn't know the team or have any connection with them. I didn't need to have an ongoing relationship with them. It didn't matter if they became angry at me—I was just the messenger; I could walk out of their building and probably never see them again.

As a leader, 99% of the time you will be the one offering *your* feedback and receiving feedback from *your* people within *your* team and organisation. You will have a connection with them. You will (hopefully) know the names of their loved ones. You may have recruited them. You *need* to have an ongoing relationship with them. If you think there is a risk of a conversation going pear-shaped, it's understandable you will want to avoid that conversation.

In many cases, the risks of having feedback conversations are high and immediate, but the risk of not having those feedback conversations are even higher and have longer-term negative consequences. When you don't have the conversations that it would be useful for the organisation to have, you miss opportunities to learn and grow and, therefore, improve performance. A Feedback Fit culture drives performance.

As a leader, you are walking the tightrope of backing yourself and your decisions—and also being open to other people's opinions and feedback. You might be in danger of becoming a people-pleaser—not wanting to upset anyone, ever. You might have been taught, 'If you haven't anything nice to say, don't say anything at all,' and yet here you are, in a leadership role in which it is your job to sometimes say things that could be perceived as 'not nice'.

Here are more examples of fears and concerns leaders have shared with me privately in regard to feedback conversations and maintaining ongoing relationships:

- 'What if they become upset or angry or withdrawn?'
- 'What if I offer them feedback and they think I'm being a bitch/bastard?'
- 'They can make my life a living hell—she is meant to be sharing her knowledge with me so I can do my job. I'm worried that if I upset her, she won't.'
- 'I want them to like me, actually I *need* them to like me.'
- 'I want team harmony not hostility.'
- 'It's a small town and I'm married to her sister . . .'
- 'I really like him/her, I don't want to upset him/her.'
- 'We were peers and friends outside of work, and then I stepped up into a team leader role. It's tricky.'

Some leaders pride themselves on being approachable, inclusive, and collaborative. They can also be over-responsible for the emotions of their team members and don't want any 'negative' feedback they offer to upset anyone. They believe their feedback can 'make others feel uncomfortable', and they don't want to do that because it's *awkward*.

When it comes to receiving feedback, many people are also worried about what other people think of them:

- 'I don't want to let my leader down, after all, she recruited me.'
- 'What if I'm exposed as a fraud?'
- 'I'll feel embarrassed by my mistakes/failures.'
- 'Oh God! She's called my latest project "excellent", now all my future projects must be to the same high-standard and I just don't have the energy for that . . .'
- 'My leader thinks I'm dumb/stupid . . .'
- 'It's only a matter of time before my leader realises I'm not as good as s/he thinks I am.'
- 'I don't want to disappoint them, my team, anyone (everyone, ever).'

Your organisation has a 'nice and polite' culture

▶▶ *One person's story: An anonymous CEO*

The following was said to me by one of the CEOs I coached:

> When it comes to feedback, we have an avoidance culture. Leaders would rather be perceived as 'nice' and 'polite'. Sometimes it's just easier to not say anything. But in the car park, plenty is being said about people behind their backs.

When I asked this CEO to tell me more, she shared that her organisation hadn't invested in its people or created a healthy feedback culture. The leaders hadn't had any training on the topic of feedback.

> To be fair, the skills just aren't there. As a result, the conversations are not being had, and the expectations are not clear. But it's more than that, we have an avoidance culture.

Suppose an organisation has done the groundwork and developed systems to ensure a Feedback Fit culture was in place—a culture in which feedback conversations were expected and normal. Suppose this started at the recruitment phase, was included in interviews, and then was part of the 'onboarding' process:

Welcome to the team. We value your learning, growth and ongoing development. We have many conversations in which we offer and receive feedback from each other. Don't worry, we will ensure you possess the skills to have these conversations.

Ensure there are no surprises, just clear expectations, with a clear process and conversations about that process. Importantly, encourage people to see the value of feedback conversations, and to be actively contributing to a culture of Feedback Fitness. You might need to 'sell' the benefits to them!

FEEDBACK *Fitness*

Word on the Street

Survey question

I asked a sample of people the following question:

> What do you believe are the barriers to leaders offering feedback in the workplace?

The responses have been grouped into the following four main themes.

i Leaders are worried about how it will go.
ii Leaders are lacking in skill/confidence.
iii Leaders have time constraints.
iv The organisation's systems and culture do not support Feedback Fitness.

I will now discuss each of these themes in more detail.

(i) Leaders are worried about how it will go

The following list summarises how this was expressed by the survey participants.

- Not wanting to upset staff.
- Worried about how it will be received.
- Worried the recipient will get offended/upset.
- Fear of impact on staff (for example, making them upset or anxious).
- Worried about how it will be received by employees (especially older, more established employees).
- Fear of how staff may receive the feedback, especially if it has been anticipated as negative.
- Worried about giving negative or constructive feedback because unsure of the response.
- Negative reactions from reports/fear.
- Fear of offending/hurting others, and the reactions that could result.
- Concerned about the reaction and repercussions that may occur.

- 'Direct reports' feeling personally attacked and not receptive to feedback.
- Concerns about how to best offer constructive feedback.
- Fear of getting it wrong or making things worse.
- Fear of doing it wrong.
- Not saying the right thing.
- Insecurity.
- A lack of psychological safety.
- Not wanting conflict.
- Fear and an inability to invest in the relationship outside of giving feedback.
- Trying to maintain respect from employees.
- Worried it will lead to low morale.
- It will at times be taken the wrong way and seen as 'power over' or 'bullying'.
- Upsetting the harmony in the workplace.
- Knowledge that it won't be accepted.
- Rejection and disbelief.
- The lack of resilience from others in receiving the feedback.
- Having a history of not doing it and the worry of staff leaving if it is done.

(ii) Leaders are lacking in skill/confidence

The following list summarises how this was expressed by the survey participants.

- Leaders are not skilled in offering feedback and are rather clumsy at offering it.
- Not sure how to do it in a sensitive way.
- Not sure how to ensure feedback is actionable.
- Not knowing how to offer feedback that is relevant and specific, while setting expectations.
- Not enough experience.
- They don't have the necessary skills.

- Lack of feedback training/experience.
- Lack of knowledge in relation to how and when.
- Lack of experience/understanding related to how to offer feedback.
- Lack of confidence or not knowing how to deliver the feedback.
- Lack of management capability in people-management skills, leading to a lack of confidence to have honest feedback conversations.
- Unsure what to say, how to say it, lack of relationship to offer feedback, lack of well-defined expectations/goals to measure against.
- Insecurity of abilities, self-doubt, fear of judgement.
- Not confident—lack of practice/guidance to build the necessary skills.
- Unclear themselves on the expectations and how to hold people accountable.
- Lack of confidence and awareness of the importance of feedback.

(iii) Leaders have time constraints

The following list summarises how this was expressed by the survey participants.

- Lack of time 'x 8'.
- Perceived lack of time.
- Time to structure, deliver and seek feedback; everything is always 'urgent' and opportunities for feedback are forever pushed to 'later'.
- Time needed to have one-on-one conversations, so feedback can be given sensitively and with appropriate time for the recipient to digest and respond.
- Lack of time and an abundance of work.
- They just don't make the time.
- Time poor (don't schedule time to give feedback).
- Time and the confidence to provide feedback.
- Time poor and not understanding roles.
- Time constraints; see it as optional; lack of confidence.

- Time-poor, no appropriate set-up.
- Lack of time; limited knowledge on how to offer feedback.
- Time to prepare and the busy nature of our workplace.
- Lack of available time, not being in the same location as the team.
- Having enough time to reflect on the work of individuals; have so many people in teams and extremely busy.
- Poor communication/insufficient time for feedback to occur.
- Needs continuity, taking the time to evaluate staff performance and communicate.

(iv) The organisation's systems and culture do not support Feedback Fitness

The following list summarises how this was expressed by the survey participants.

- Clunky/ineffective performance review process.
- 'Us and them' syndrome.
- The culture hasn't been set up for staff to be able to receive feedback in a timely manner.
- Not being held accountable by their leaders to provide feedback.
- Lack of clarity around expectations of what good performance looks like within and across teams.
- Tradition and culture; the way things are done around here—set by the leader.
- Personality types—some are very open, others very closed.
- Lack of processes implemented.

3
Feedback Fitness Framework

Overview of the Feedback Fitness framework

Moving on from the 'sh*t sandwich'

When I ask people to name feedback frameworks, the most common answer I am given is 'the sh*t sandwich'. Basically, this is a framework involving the offering of feedback in the following format:

- start with offering 'positive' feedback
- offer the 'negative' feedback
- then finish with offering more 'positive' feedback.

This is not a useful way to offer feedback because everyone's brain tends to remember the start and the end of a conversation, more than it does the middle. If you are taking the time to offer someone feedback, you want them to remember the middle!

> ··· What Dr Adam Grant says ···
>
> Here is what popular organisational psychologist Dr Adam Grant says about the 'sh*t sandwich':
>
> *It doesn't help to bury criticism between two compliments: The feedback sandwich doesn't taste as good as it looks. Beginnings and ends are more likely to stick in our memories than middles...*[17]

When delivered poorly, the 'sandwich' approach can sound fake and scripted. It's in danger of being confusing instead of clear, and it certainly doesn't feel like a two-way conversation. It feels like a cop-out—trying to 'hide' the feedback between two 'nice' comments and seeming like the person offering the feedback is fearful of how that feedback will be received. I'm guilty in this regard—I've offered this type of sandwich in the past to people I have led, and it was an unpleasant experience for all involved!

Welcome to the next version of feedback!

The Feedback Fitness framework provides a structure to be used in feedback conversations. It is not a script. It is a process that allows you to know where you are in a conversation without sounding fake or forced.

The Feedback Fitness framework consists of three steps:

1 the warm-up
2 the workout
3 the cool-down

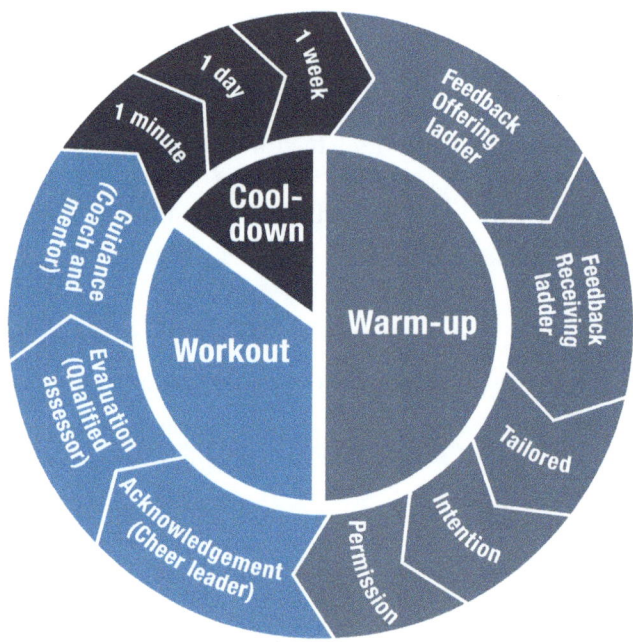

1 The warm-up conversation

Just as you wouldn't go straight into running a 100-metre sprint, in running spikes and using starting blocks, without first doing an extensive complete warm-up, don't offer feedback without first doing a full warm-up—especially if you want to have an ongoing relationship with the other person.

For world-class athletes, a 100-metre sprint usually takes around 9.5–11 seconds. Athletes spend years training to develop the skills necessary for achieving that. On the day of a competition, some of them can spend about 90 minutes warming up, getting their minds and bodies ready to perform at their best. That 90-minute warm-up can be referred to as a 'full' warm-up.

The same applies to feedback conversations. You can spend years developing your communication and leadership skills, but you still need to do a full warm-up, preparing both you and the other person, before commencing a feedback conversation. But you don't have to do an extensive, full 90-minute warm up conversation every time you want to offer feedback! In the case of feedback conversations, the full warm-up is a one-off conversation that sets the foundations for all the other, in-the-moment, regular feedback conversations that will happen for the rest of the year.

2 The workout conversations

The workout is the part of the Feedback Fitness framework in which the feedback offering and feedback receiving conversations take place. It is made up of three subsections, which allow you to be very clear on the type of feedback you are offering, the purpose for that feedback, and the role into which you are stepping.

It helps you to be prepared and deliberate. The approach is super easy to remember and you don't need to offer all three types of feedback in *every* feedback conversation—you probably won't have time for that!

The workout phase helps you to feel confident in offering deliberate, clear and actionable feedback.

3 The cool-down conversations

As for sprinters, it is important to recover well so you can perform again and are not sore the next day. The cool-down for athletes is usually a slow jog, stretching, rehydration, nutrition, and maybe even a massage. The cool-down is all about wellbeing—recovery, reducing any soreness and avoiding risk of injury.

A cool-down is also important for feedback conversations. It is about reducing the likelihood of damaging relationships and ensuring continuous improvement in performance. The cool-down is led by the person who offers the feedback. It has three stages which are, again, super easy to remember.

As was the case for the warm-up and the workout, you don't need to have a cool-down conversation *every* time you offer feedback.

Sounds like a lot of work, and I'm already flat out

Have you ever turned up late for an exercise class and thought, 'I don't need to do a warm-up; I'll just jump straight in—it'll be all right'? Or, at the conclusion of a workout, when you know you should do a cool-down, have you ever skipped it because you are busy? You might even have promised yourself you would do it when you got home (but you didn't)!

I understand you are busy—let's set up your feedback conversations so they can be frequent and flowing. You don't have time for friction and f*ck-ups!

Is it possible to sprint 100 metres without doing a full warm-up or cool-down? Sure it is. But the risks are that you are more likely to injure yourself; you won't perform at your best; and your recovery will be compromised. You will be at an increased risk of tearing your hamstring and being out of action for 6–8 weeks. It is also likely that you will spend time and money trying to repair the damage that could have been avoided.

The same applies to feedback conversations. The temptation is to jump right in and offer the feedback (get it over with), without really knowing how it's going to go—just crossing your fingers and hoping for the best. After all, we are all super busy! Who has time for full warm-up and cool-down conversations . . . right? The more useful question is, if a feedback conversation goes pear-shaped, who has time for damage control, replacing someone who has resigned, or dealing with a complaint to HR or a bullying claim?

▶▶ One person's story: An anonymous workshop participant

I was delivering the Feedback Fitness workshop to a team of thirty government engineers. When I started explaining the metaphor, 'You wouldn't sprint 100 metres without warming up first.' One participant replied:

> *You are right, I wouldn't sprint 100 metres! I haven't exercised since 1997!*

The exercise metaphor hadn't worked for him.

What did work for him was to replace 'warm-up' with 'preparation and planning', 'workout' with 'implementation', and 'cool-down' with 'review.'

Whatever works for you!

4
Introduction to the Warm-up Conversation

A leader once asked me for help. He told me when he offered feedback to a team member, he/she would 'get their back up and get all defensive and take it personally'.

My response was: 'Have you had a warm-up conversation in which you talk *about* feedback, before you offer any feedback?'

The importance of a full warm-up conversation *before* offering feedback

A warm-up conversation is the name for what occurs when you have a conversation about feedback before you offer or receive any feedback. You ask the other person what their beliefs are about feedback. You discuss often unspoken topics, including your feedback styles, expectations, preferences, experiences and intentions.

There are many good reasons why it's worth investing in warm-up conversations.

Going 'upstream'

You may be familiar with Dan Heath's book, *Upstream: The quest to solve problems before they happen*,[18] about the power of foreseeing a problem and identifying it at the source, so the likelihood of that problem occurring in the future can be reduced. Heath uses the metaphor of preventing issues at the source by 'going upstream', rather than dealing with a continual flow of issues once they have reached points further 'downstream'.

What has this to do with warm-up conversations?

When you can foresee a potential problem, (such as feedback conversations going pear-shaped), you have more manoeuvring room to avoid or reduce the associated risks. The problem in many organisations is not feedback, it's the fear of emotions resulting from feedback conversations, and then avoidance of feedback conversations to avoid the emotions! The invisible cost of fear and avoidance of feedback conversations is enormous. I wish I could put a dollar figure on it!

How to go 'upstream' in feedback conversations

Warm-up conversations allow us to foresee potential problems that could eventuate from offering and receiving feedback *before* they occur. Use a warm-up conversation to talk *about* feedback, and to identify patterns and trends in the other person's feedback beliefs and behaviour. Does that person have a history of taking feedback personally? Ask them about their past and recent feedback experiences. Invite them to go 'upstream' with you, so you can both avoid rough waters 'downstream'.

The warm-up conversation is where you set the stage for all future feedback conversations. It is an investment for everyone involved and increases psychological safety, for both you and the other person.

Types of warm-up conversations

There are two types of warm-up conversations: full warm-up conversations; and pre-frame warm-up conversations.

1 Full warm-up conversations
   - Occur once or twice a year.
   - Last 60–90 minutes.
   - Discuss feedback in general terms, without raising specific instances.

2 Pre-frame warm-up conversations
   - Brief, one-sentence warm-ups, delivered right before offering feedback.
   - These warm-ups set the intention and encourage 'buy-in'.

> ▶▶ *Sneak peek: Example of a pre-frame warm-up* ....

A pre-frame warm-up could be approached in a manner similar to this:

> Hey Olivia, can I share something I have noticed about the wording of your email to the senior leadership group, because I know you care about how you come across to them?

We will explore the structure of the pre-frame warm-up conversation in detail in Chapter 7, 'Introduction to the Workout Conversation' (see page 75).

How to initiate a full warm-up conversation

You can have full warm-up conversations as one-on-one conversations, have them as a team, or both. Ideally, the warm-up process starts at the recruitment stage:

> *Come join our team. We value your development and growth. We have a culture in which feedback conversations are expected and welcomed. Honesty and respect are important to us. If you join our team, you will be involved in conversations for which you are both offering and receiving feedback on a regular basis. Interested?*

During a recruitment interview

Ask your potential team member:

- ▸ 'What's important to you about feedback in the workplace?'
- ▸ 'Can you share a time when you received feedback that helped your performance to improve?'
- ▸ 'Can you think of an example of a work-related situation in which it took courage to offer the feedback you did?'

As part of the standard onboarding process

Include warm-up conversations similar to the following as part of the standard onboarding process:

> *Congratulations and welcome to our team! In our team we promote a culture in which feedback conversations are regular*

and expected. We value honesty and respect. There will be no surprises in our feedback conversations. In a few weeks, when you have settled into the role/team, we will talk more about feedback. That way we will both be clear on expectations.

With a new team member

When a person is new to the team (or you as leader are new to the team), it's beneficial to have a warm-up conversation as soon as possible—but not on the first day, because that might be a little overwhelming! Once you have established connections and trust, have a warm-up conversation one-on-one, in a location where you both feel comfortable talking about feedback. Remember you are not offering any feedback yet, just talking *about* future feedback conversations.

With your existing team

Let's say you have a pretty solid team with no recent new members. You can initiate warm-up conversations at any time, be it individually during regular one-on-one catch-ups/supervision, or as part of team meetings. You could embed these conversations into a future team/strategic planning day.

▶▶ *One person's story: Jessie*

The following is what one leader, Jessie, shared about her approach:

> *I invited the whole team to a one-hour conversation about the feedback culture of our team. I made 'Feedback Conversations' the only topic on the agenda. I was careful to add an explanation to the invitation explaining the meeting was about how we can improve our feedback conversations. I knew if I didn't do that, some people would automatically freak out and assume I had BIG FEEDBACK for them and had called a SPECIAL meeting! Together we talked through the Offering and Receiving ladders [more on these ladders next]. Then we used the 'Fifty Questions about Feedback' cards provided by Sue Anderson. It went really well. We could have kept talking. I learnt more about my team in one hour than I have learnt about them over the last 12 months.*

The warm-up process

The warm-up conversation has five components: two different self-assessment measures (the Feedback Offering ladder and the Feedback Receiving ladder [see Chapter 5, 'Feedback Self-assessments'), and my three 'TIPs' (an acronym for '**T**ailored; **I**ntention; **P**ermission' [see Chapter 6, 'Three Feedback TIPs']). These are represented diagrammatically below.

You don't need to remember these five elements, but you might like to print the free resources from my website (https://www.sue-anderson.com.au) and use them as part of your warm-up conversations.

If meeting with someone one-on-one, sit alongside the other person (not opposite them) and take them through the five components of the warm-up. Ask questions and listen to their responses, without judging or correcting them. One of the outcomes of the full warm-up conversation is gaining a greater understanding of the other person and their belief system regarding feedback.

Model a Feedback Fit person to them by sharing your thoughts and feelings about feedback. Be aware of any power dynamics between the two of you and, importantly, be sure to lead the conversation from a place of trust and compassion.

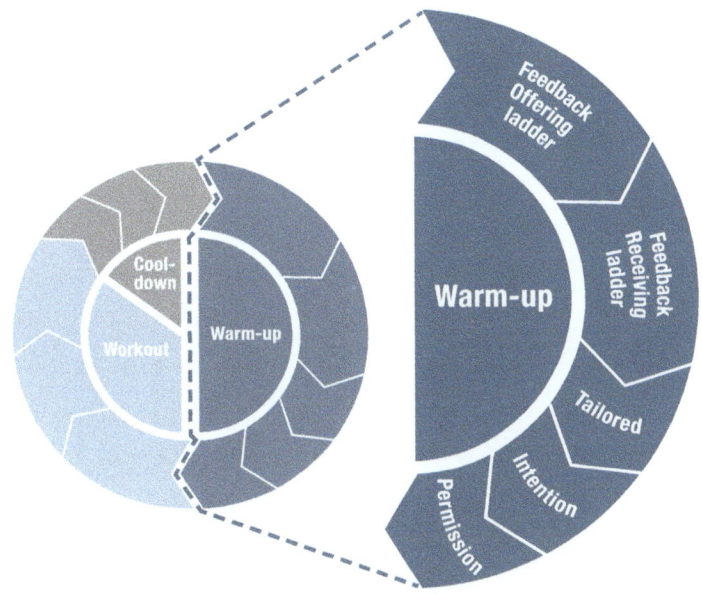

What Dr Libby Brook says

Dr Libby Brook is an organisational psychologist and expert in psychological health and safety. Here is what she has said about the warm-up conversation:

> *The warm-up is about understanding what the other person wants, their needs and what makes them comfortable with feedback. There's also trustworthiness and transparency to consider. You can use the warm-up to create trust, and it's important to have a level of trust in the first place.*

> *The warm-up is about transparency and setting expectations because you're talking about what you're going to do, how we're going to shape it, what it's going to look like and how it's going to go. It's really about helping the other person to feel empowered with some control, so they have some choice in the situation. Help people to feel as comfortable as possible to reduce their stress response.*[19]

5
Feedback Self-assessments

Let's start by considering two of the Feedback Fitness framework's self-assessment tools, which take the form of two simple ladders: the Feedback Offering ladder; and the Feedback Receiving ladder. The idea is that we can all, easily and quickly, identify where we are (in general terms) on each of the ladders. Keep in mind that you do move up and down these ladders at different times, so we are speaking *generally* when we locate ourselves on a ladder. The ladders are aspirational, meaning you want to be working your way up them over time.

But, before we get to the ladders, let's encourage your team to start talking about feedback in a psychologically safe way.

Make friends with offering feedback

Discuss the offering of feedback with your team in a light and breezy way. Have fun with it. You might feel comfortable sharing a story from your own 'interesting' feedback experiences. Have a laugh about awkward feedback you have been offered (or have offered).

Use any number of the following questions to encourage your team to talk about offering feedback.

1. 'What do you believe about feedback in general?'
2. 'What is one thing about offering feedback that "lights you up"?'
3. 'What holds you back from offering feedback?'
4. 'What is your feedback offering style?'
5. 'If you were going to model yourself on someone who is highly skilled at offering feedback, who would that be?'
6. 'How do you know when the feedback you offer is received well?'

7. 'Are you offering enough feedback? How do you know?'
8. 'What is your worst feedback offering moment?'
9. 'What is your best feedback offering moment?'
10. 'What is your approach when offering feedback to someone who is more senior than you?'
11. 'How do you offer feedback to your (line) manager?'
12. 'In what way, if any, did your family talk about offering feedback when you were growing up?'
13. 'What could your grandparents teach you about offering feedback?'
14. 'How do you feel when you offer someone feedback, but they choose not to listen?'
15. 'How do you balance being honest with being kind when offering feedback?'
16. 'What is one thing you admire about how others offer feedback?'
17. 'Who would you never offer feedback to?'
18. 'When is offering "in the moment" feedback not okay with you?'
19. 'How often do you offer feedback to your peers/colleagues?'
20. 'What is your approach for offering feedback to someone more junior than you?'
21. 'How would you describe the feedback offering culture in your team and organisation?'
22. 'How do you make sure the feedback you offer is actionable?'
23. 'If you could offer feedback to someone famous, who would it be and what would your feedback be?'
24. 'What feedback would you offer your clone (and would your clone take it on board)?'
25. 'Have you ever given up offering feedback to someone? What was your reasoning?'

26 'What strategies could you use to offer feedback to someone who usually becomes defensive?'

27 'What do you believe about offering anonymous feedback to others?'

28 'What do you believe about offering someone "a sh*t sandwich"?'

29 'What feedback are you passionate about offering?'

30 'Out of ten, how would you rate your feedback offering skills?'

31 'What is your earliest workplace feedback offering memory?'

32 'Do you believe workplace feedback is best offered publicly, or privately?'

33 'What is the best feedback offering advice you have ever received?'

34 'What is the worst feedback offering advice you have ever received?'

35 'What is your general experience of offering feedback to others?'

36 'Have you ever been guilty of offering "drive-by" feedback? What was the circumstance?'

37 'Have you ever "feedback-bombed" anyone?'

38 'In your opinion, do you believe feedback offered online is as useful as feedback offered face-to-face?'

39 'What type of emotions do you experience when offering feedback?'

40 'How do you ensure you offer psychologically safe feedback?'

Three key questions about offering feedback

If time is limited, ask your team members only these three key questions:

- 'What do you believe about offering feedback?'
- 'What's important to you about offering feedback?'
- 'What does offering feedback mean to you?'

The Feedback Offering self-assessment

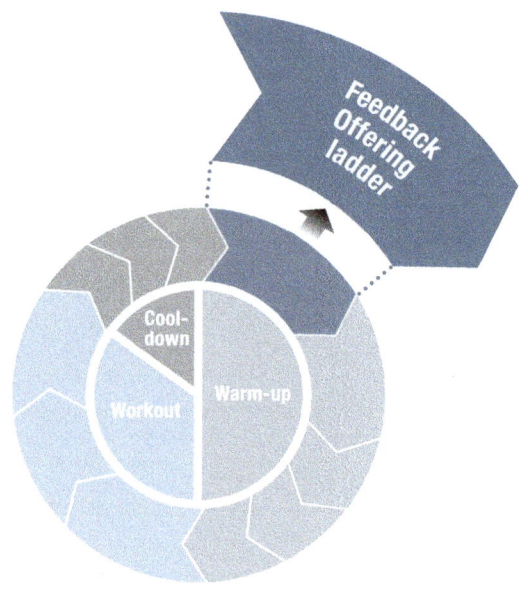

The Feedback Offering ladder

How you feel when offering feedback	Performance
Courageous	80–99%
Confident	60–80%
Comfortable	40–60%
Clumsy	20–40%
Confused	0–20%

To indicate how they feel when offering feedback, ask your team members to place themselves on the Feedback Offering ladder (above), in general terms and in the context of the team of which they are *now* a part.

If this is done in a team meeting, they might not want to share openly. But, if there is enough trust and rapport in the team, they might.

Following are some characteristics associated with people who place themselves on different rungs of the Feedback Offering ladder.

Confused

- They actively avoid having to offer feedback, unless there is no choice.
- They will ask a third person to 'give' feedback on their behalf.
- They use no framework or process, (maybe offering the 'sh*t sandwich').
- They fill silences with vague statements, or judgements, or by repeatedly apologising.
- They focus on themselves.
- They shut the other person down if they try to speak.
- They ask zero questions.
- They end the conversation (if there is one) as quickly as possible.
- They avoid the recipient of their feedback for the next three weeks, because it is 'awkward'.
- They do not follow-up; instead they pretend that the conversation never happened.

Clumsy

- They typically try not to offer feedback—it is just 'too risky'.
- They are not sure where to start, what words to use, or when is a good time.
- They avoid feedback conversations whenever possible.
- They are not good listeners.
- They are unaware of any framework or process for offering feedback.
- They fill silences by talking, apologising or talking about themselves.
- They often deliver a speech, with no questions.
- They do not follow up.

Comfortable

- They believe they have a degree of feedback offering skills.
- They offer feedback in the way in which they like to receive it.
- They are guided by a framework.
- They initiate feedback conversations about half of the time.
- They have some listening skills.
- They try to determine the best time and place for the conversation.
- They allow for some silences and hold the space for the other person to respond.
- They use a few questions.
- They may follow-up with the person at the next one-on-one conversation.

Confident

- They feel confident they have good quality feedback offering skills.
- They mostly tailor the feedback to the other person's preferences for receiving feedback.
- They are loosely guided by a framework, but the feedback is mostly conversational.
- They initiate feedback conversations most of the time.
- They have good listening skills.
- They are mostly skilled at determining the best time and place for the conversation.
- They allow for silences, holding the space for the other person to respond.
- They use deliberate questions.
- They actively follow up with the other person.

Courageous

- They have the courage to have even the most challenging feedback conversations.
- They always tailor the feedback to the other person's preferences.

- They are guided by a framework *and* feedback is conversational.
- They initiate feedback conversations whenever possible.
- They have advanced listening skills.
- They are skilled at determining the best time and place for the conversation.
- They allow for silences to hold the space, enabling the other person to respond.
- They have a system in place to actively follow up with the other person after the conversation.

The way you think about offering feedback

How you think about offering feedback holds your feedback offering behaviour in place.

▶▶ One person's story: Bek

Bek rated herself as 'Confident' on the Feedback Offering ladder. The beliefs she expressed about feedback were useful:

> Offering feedback is part of my leadership role and helps my team members to improve and provide excellent services for our clients. Finding the balance between care and compassion and holding them accountable can be tricky. I want to encourage my team and, at the same time, hold them accountable. I also want to be a better leader for them. I sometimes ask them for feedback on my feedback.

▶▶ One person's story: Jon

Jon rated himself as 'Clumsy' on the Feedback Offering ladder. His beliefs about feedback influenced his feedback offering behaviour:

> I consider giving feedback as dangerous and risky. I've had past experiences where I provided feedback and it was later used against me. I'm afraid of saying the wrong thing, upsetting someone, or damaging a relationship I've worked hard to build. Because of this, I'm reluctant to offer feedback unless I really have to. After I give it, I go over the conversation

> *again and again in my mind trying to remember what I said and playing out worst-case scenarios, usually involving HR.*

Jon could do all the feedback giving and receiving training available but, if his belief is 'Giving feedback is dangerous and risky', his behaviour of avoiding offering feedback will remain unchanged. It's the same for all of us—to make sustainable changes in our behaviour, we need to make sure our beliefs are useful.

> **Tip:**
> Our beliefs hold our behaviour in place.

If you are avoiding offering feedback, it's worth thinking about what you are actually trying to avoid. It might not be the task of offering the feedback itself that seems hard. It is more likely a fear of the consequences if you get it wrong, and of the emotions you may experience as a result of those consequences.

> **Tip:**
> We are always trying to keep ourselves safe, and that sometimes means we justify *not* offering feedback.

'It depends'

When asked where they sit on the Feedback Offering ladder, many people respond with: 'It depends.'

When this happens, ask what specifically 'it depends' upon. The answer to that is invaluable information for you as a leader because, once the 'It depends' considerations of your team members are identified, you will be able to ensure those influences don't get in the way of your future feedback conversations.

Here are some examples of 'It depends' responses when it comes to offering feedback.

'It depends' on:
- who I'm offering the feedback to
- my relationship with them

- if there is a risk our relationship will be damaged
- what the topic is
- where we are at the time
- if they value my opinion
- if I'm qualified to comment
- if I care about the topic
- if I care about the other person
- if I can be bothered
- if they have listened in the past
- if they are open to my feedback
- if I have time
- what mood I'm in
- what mood they are in
- if they have been open to my feedback in the past
- if it is worth the risk of them taking it personally/the wrong way.

What Dr Brené Brown says

Brené Brown is an American professor and researcher; and a popular author and podcast host. She is known for her work on vulnerability and leadership and has said this about the offering of feedback:

> ... to not give people feedback, to not be truthful, to not do the hard coaching that we have to do as leaders, because we don't want to hurt people's feelings is kind of bullshit... [W]e're hiding behind that to minimize our own discomfort. And there's nothing more devastating for people than not getting feedback... [W]hen I don't give you feedback for growth, it's almost like I'm saying to you, 'I don't believe that you can get better, or stronger, or be a better leader. It's not worth my time.' And that's hard.[20]

Ouch! It felt like Brené Brown punched me in the stomach when I first read this quote. Let's use Kristin Neff's research findings and apply some self-kindness here![21]

It makes sense that we want to protect ourselves from perceived danger. In fact, we are wired to do that. If you, like many other leaders, have been exposed to only limited modelling of quality feedback offering skills, the only framework you might be aware of is the 'sh*t sandwich'. If you are walking into feedback conversations blindly, not sure how they are going to go, it makes total sense that you would try to keep yourself safe from perceived danger.

If you can relate to the situation just described, you are not alone. A Harris Poll research study showed: 'Over a third (37%) of the managers said that they're uncomfortable having to give direct feedback about their employees' performance if they think the employee might respond negatively to the feedback.'[22] My guess is that they would be more comfortable if they had a structure ensuring they were not going into the conversation blind in regard to how it might play out.

▶▶ *One person's story: An anonymous leader*

A leader I coached expressed the following realisation:

> *No wonder I avoided giving feedback all these years. My experience was it usually ended badly. Now I realise I have never done a warm-up; I have just gone straight in, stated the feedback and hoped for the best. I've been walking into the unknown.*

Let's change that! It doesn't need to happen to you.

Make friends with receiving feedback

Part of the warm-up conversation will include talking about receiving feedback. We will explore the receiving of feedback more in the second half of this book, but it's included here because it is a key ingredient of the warm-up conversation.

You may like to encourage your team to talk about their experiences of receiving feedback by using the following questions to generate discussion. You will gain much insight into your team members' beliefs and attitudes towards feedback and their own roles by encouraging them to share their beliefs about receiving feedback.

Use any number of the following questions to encourage your team to talk about receiving feedback.

1. 'What's the most surprising feedback you have ever received?'
2. 'How well did you receive feedback as a teenager?'
3. 'Describe a situation in which you do not wish to receive feedback.'
4. 'Have you ever felt embarrassed, ashamed or guilty when someone offered you feedback? What did you do to work through those emotions?'
5. 'What feedback have you received that you were grateful for?'
6. 'When was the last time you actively asked for feedback?'
7. 'How do you respond to anonymous feedback?'
8. 'Are you receiving enough feedback from others? How do you know?'
9. 'If you were going to model yourself on someone who is highly skilled in receiving feedback, who would that be?'
10. 'What is the most memorable feedback you have ever received?'
11. 'What was the feedback receiving culture in your family when you were growing up?'
12. 'Have you ever pretended to take someone's feedback on board, knowing very well that you will disregard it as soon as the conversation is over?'
13. 'What are your feedback triggers (if any)?'
14. 'How much feedback did you receive as a child?'
15. 'Have you ever received feedback that was not actionable? What did you do?'
16. 'How would you describe the feedback receiving culture in your team and organisation?'
17. 'If you could bring one person back to life and ask them for feedback, who would it be?'

18 'What is one thing about receiving feedback that scares you?'
19 'Out of ten, how would you rate your feedback receiving skills?'
20 'What is one crucial ingredient that helps you to receive feedback well?'
21 'If you have your own children, what have you taught them about receiving feedback?'
22 'What could your grandparents teach you about receiving feedback?'
23 'If you could offer one piece of advice to a large group of people about receiving feedback, what would it be?'
24 'What is one piece of feedback you were offered in the past that you wish you had implemented?'
25 'What kind of feedback do you find most useful to receive—acknowledgement, evaluation or guidance?'
26 'How do you handle receiving feedback from someone with whom you don't get along?'
27 'What is the most beautiful feedback you have ever been offered?'
28 'How do you know when you have been offered really useful feedback? What is your evidence?'
29 'What is the funniest feedback you have ever been offered?'
30 'Describe your best feedback receiving moment.'
31 'Share your worst feedback receiving moment.'
32 'What is important to you about receiving feedback?'
33 'Who would you never accept feedback from?'
34 'What is one thing you expect when receiving feedback?'
35 'What is one of your favourite things about receiving feedback?'
36 'When has feedback made you smile?'
37 'Do you like being offered "in-the-moment" feedback? What does it depend on?'
38 'Have you ever received feedback that felt like "a punch in the guts"?'

39 'What is your preferred feedback receiving language?'

40 'What was the most recent feedback you received?'

41 'What is your earliest workplace feedback receiving memory?'

42 'What feedback do you miss from your past?'

43 'What is a topic you would like more feedback on?'

44 'What is something you recently discovered about yourself through someone offering you feedback?'

45 'From which famous person would you like to receive feedback?'

46 'What feedback have you received that sticks in your memory the most?'

47 'What do you believe is the worst way to receive feedback?'

48 'What do you believe about receiving feedback from your colleagues?'

49 'Have you ever been a victim of "drive-by" feedback? How did you respond?'

50 'Have you ever been "feedback-bombed"? How did you respond?'

Three key questions about receiving feedback

If time is limited, ask your team members only these three key questions:

- 'What do you believe about receiving feedback?'
- 'What's important to you about receiving feedback?'
- 'What does receiving feedback mean to you?'

The Feedback Receiving self-assessment

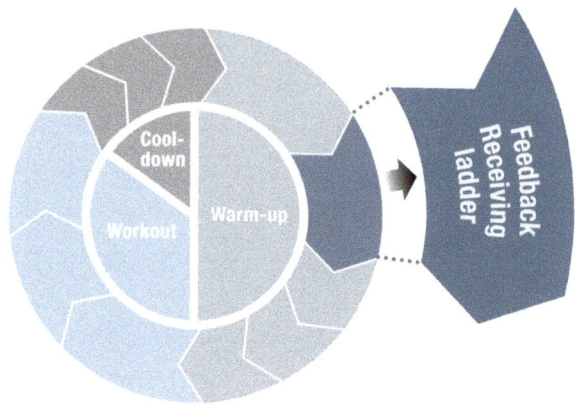

The Feedback Receiving ladder

How you feel when receiving feedback	Openness to receiving feedback
Resilient	80–99%
Receptive	60–80%
Reluctant	40–60%
Resistant	20–40%
Rejecting	0–20%

To indicate how they feel when receiving feedback, ask your team members to place themselves on the Feedback Receiving ladder (above), in general terms and in the context of the team of which they are *now* a part.

If this is done in a team meeting, they might not want to share openly. But, as for the Feedback Offering discussion, if there is enough trust and rapport in the team, they might.

Following are some characteristics associated with people who place themselves on different rungs of the Feedback Receiving ladder.

Rejecting

- These people are closed to all feedback.
- They are defensive, dismissive, and often disengaged.
- They take feedback as a personal attack.
- They are not open to considering the feedback and just reject it.
- Their performance is poor.

Resistant

- These people are fearful of feedback and would rather not receive it.
- They have no interest in learning or growing.
- They will often ignore feedback, even if it is repeated many times.
- Their performance is consistently average at best.

Reluctant

- These people vary in their openness to receiving feedback—'it depends' upon their stress levels.
- Often, they dread receiving feedback but, on reflection, then are grateful and see it as beneficial.
- Their performance is inconsistent.

Receptive

- These people often request feedback.
- They believe feedback can be very useful.
- They don't take feedback personally and see it as part of their learning process.
- Their performance is good, and they are looking for ways to continually improve.

Resilient

- Feedback resilient people actively seek out feedback, with the intention of using it to develop their skills, learn and grow. They use it for motivation, focus and clarity.

- They consider all feedback received and then filter it for usefulness, respectfully disregarding what is not useful to them.
- They strive for excellence and value and they appreciate feedback.
- Their performance and effort are excellent.

The way you think about receiving feedback

Where are you and your team members on the Feedback Receiving ladder?

▶▶ *One person's story: Jo*

> Jo leads a team of three and provided the following information:
>
> *Sarah, who has been in the team the longest, is very open to and loves feedback. She asks me for feedback on a regular basis, in a growth way, not in a needy, validation-seeking way. I've noticed Sarah picks up on my tone and body language as much as the actual words I use.*
>
> *Then there's Priya. I'd consider Priya a bit reluctant to [receive] my feedback and [she] can take it personally at times. It's a bit hit-and-miss. She will take Sarah's feedback on board, but really struggles with feedback from our customers.*
>
> *Chris is basically uncoachable and unleadable. He does not take feedback at all, although he says he does. Actually, that's an exaggeration. He loves positive feedback. When I try to give him constructive feedback, he doesn't listen. [H]e just starts offering me feedback, and kind of hijacks the conversation. I don't think he respects me as a leader. I'm getting to the stage where I'm thinking of going to HR to get advice around starting performance management conversations. I dread having to do that, but I kind of feel stuck.*

If you lead a team of five people, and you have one on each of the five different levels of the Feedback Receiving ladder, it would be useful to know that *before* you offer them feedback.

'It depends' responses are useful

Just as was the case when using the Feedback Offering ladder, people will often say 'It depends' when asked where they sit on the Feedback Receiving ladder. Perfect! This is not a bad thing; this is useful. We want to know what someone's 'it depends' are. These are their criteria for what feedback they will be open to in the future

When this happens, you can again ask what specifically 'it depends' upon, to quickly gain insight into their beliefs and preferences about *receiving* feedback.

Here are some examples of 'It depends' with which people responded when they were asked about receiving feedback.

'It depends' on:

- who is offering the feedback
- my relationship with them
- whether there is a risk our relationship will be damaged if I disagree with their feedback
- where we are at the time
- if I value their opinion
- if they are qualified to comment
- if I care about the topic
- if I care about the other person
- if I have time
- what mood I'm in
- what mood they are in
- whether the last time I implemented their feedback it was helpful, or not.

What 'It depends' responders do you have in your team? For example, in a team of three, there might be:

- David, who cares about who the person offering the feedback is and their qualifications ('It depends on who is offering it').
- Adele, who makes no 'It depends' response—she takes on board all feedback, from everyone, without any filter or quality checking (which is not very useful).

▸ Rakhi who has made five thousand 'It depends' responses. You may find Rakhi very difficult to offer feedback to (unless, of course, you have a warm-up conversation)!

For some people to be convinced of your feedback, for example Ali (see the conversation below), they need to be provided with evidence of its usefulness.

▶▶ A conversation with Ali

You: 'In the context of your role, where do you rate yourself (in general) on the Feedback Receiving ladder?'

Ali: 'It depends.'

You: 'What does it depend on?'

Ali: 'If the person offering it can back up what they are saying.'

You: 'How could they back up what they are saying?'

Ali: 'I'd need to hear concrete examples, with data and facts—not just their opinion.'

You: 'How many concrete examples with data and facts?'

Ali: 'At least three.'

After a conversation like that, you have insight into why Ali says 'It depends'. It sounds like she is convinced by evidence. So, the next time you are preparing to offer Ali feedback, come prepared with three concrete examples and 'slam dunk' with data and facts.

Other people, like Damian (see the conversation below), need very actionable feedback.

▶▶ A conversation with Damian

You: 'In the context of your role, where do you rate yourself (in general), on the Feedback Receiving ladder?'

Damian: 'It depends.'

You: 'What does it depend on?'

Damian: 'It depends whether it's stuff within my control. Don't come at me with feedback about stuff happening at a management level or that's to do with suppliers. There's nothing I can do about it, so please don't waste my time. That's just frustrating.'

After a conversation like that you know, when offering feedback to Damian, that you need to talk about things within his control and acknowledge the things that are out of his control. He also has given us a little clue that time is important to him. Match him on that by using an approach like: 'Hey, Damian. Have you got a second?'

BRINGING IT TOGETHER

Have the warm-up conversations with your team members individually, or as a group. Make notes about each of their 'It depends' responses. That way, you can tailor your feedback to each of them. Remember, 'It depends' responses are a great way to keep the conversation going and to learn more about people's beliefs about receiving feedback.

Tip:
Shine a light on your feedback conversations — no more walking in blindly!

6

Three Feedback TIPs

Tailored, Intention and Permission

After you have used the two feedback self-assessments suggested for the warm-up conversation, it will be time to consider the three topics important for setting up your future feedback conversations for success. This chapter explores the finer details of the warm-up conversation and contains explanations of those three aspects that can be used during that warm-up conversation. I identify these as **T**ailored, **I**ntention and **P**ermission (and, collectively, I call them 'TIPs').

▶ **Tailored:**
Looks at how you can ask the other person about their individual feedback preferences, so you know how to offer feedback to them in the future.

▶ **Intention:**
Explores different ways you can communicate your general intention in offering feedback.

▶ **Permission:**
Explores how, out of respect to the person to whom you are offering feedback, you will ask for permission during the warm-up conversation to offer feedback, and talk about topics such as scope, agreeing to disagree, and emotions.

1 'Tailored': An overview

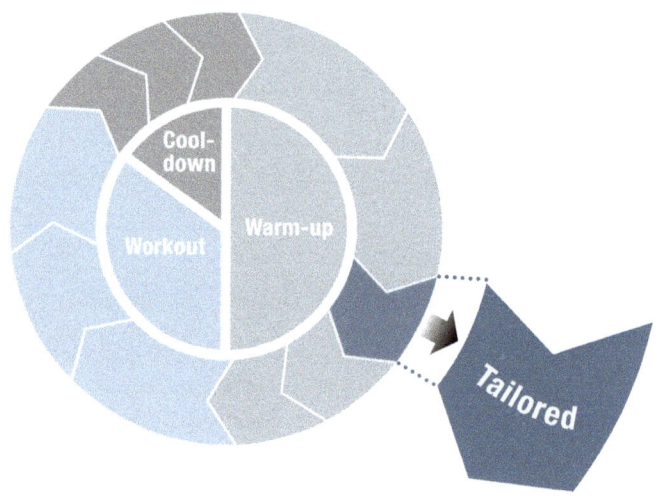

▶▶ *One person's story: An anonymous leader*

A few years ago, I coached a leader with over thirty years of leadership experience. He shared with me an 'Aha!' moment:

> *I have never thought of having warm-up conversations with my team members. In over thirty years I have never asked any of my direct reports about their beliefs about feedback. I just assumed everyone liked to receive feedback the way I do— direct and in the moment.*

In 1980, American writer Gary Chapman wrote about 'The Five Love Languages',[23] which involve concepts that do bear some relationship to the tailoring of feedback conversations to suit the person receiving the feedback. Chapman's concept of 'love languages' is that we know we are loved through different types of evidence (through words, touch, acts of service, time invested, and gifts). We all have a preference for how we want to be loved and the idea is to let your partner know your preferred love language, so they can speak yours.

You then need to find out your partner's preferred love language, so you can speak theirs. The idea is that *you* have the flexibility to speak *their* love language, even if it is not the same as your own preferred love language.

Can you see how this concept could apply to feedback conversations?

▶▶ *One person's story: Sylvia*

Sylvia loves to receive what she calls 'direct' feedback:

> *Just tell me immediately. Be honest and to the point, don't beat around the bush; give it to me straight. I'd rather know so I can fix it as soon as possible.*

▶▶ *One person's story: Liam*

In contrast to Sylvia, Liam prefers feedback that he can talk through, reflect on, and talk through again:

> *I can [be] overwhelm[ed] and not really hear what is being said. I need time to process. I don't like being put on the spot. I want time to think it over and come back to you with questions and talk about solutions and next steps.*

▶▶ *One person's story: Luna*

Luna highly values praise. When she is offered praise there is a noticeable increase in her motivation and engagement for weeks afterwards:

> *When I receive positive feedback from my peers or my leader, my confidence goes through the roof. I feel incredible! I feel like I'm floating. It means a lot to me.*

As you can see, Sylvia, Liam and Luna have different preferences for how they like to receive feedback. Know your team members' preferences before you offer them feedback.

Following are examples of some of the many ways people like to receive feedback.

- Weekly, in person, but with plenty of time to discuss.
- In person as soon as is practicable.
- In private, without notice.
- Concrete examples with evidence.
- Via email.
- Whenever, wherever.
- In the moment, in person and in private; no notice required.

The warm-up conversation provides a great opportunity for negotiating and setting clear expectations in regard to the offering and receiving of feedback.

Feedback conversations are not one-size-fits-all, so a Tailored approach requires you to ask for individual communication preferences. Some people may prefer regular, in the moment feedback, others prefer a more structured approach (for example, a scheduled, fortnightly meeting). Use the warm-up conversation as a time to negotiate and set clear expectations. Many people prefer their feedback conversations to remain confidential, others are happy to replay the conversation for anyone interested. Some people are happy to display their emotions at work, others think that is unprofessional. Discuss these kinds of considerations in the warm-up conversation.

If you ask someone about their feedback receiving preferences and they tell you they would like one hour with you every Friday afternoon so you can provide them with feedback, you might have to negotiate a compromise. For example:

> *I'd love to be able to spend that much time on your development and my schedule is pretty tight. Let's make it a scheduled thirty-minute meeting every fortnight, and I'll offer you in the moment feedback at other appropriate times.*

2 'Intention': An overview

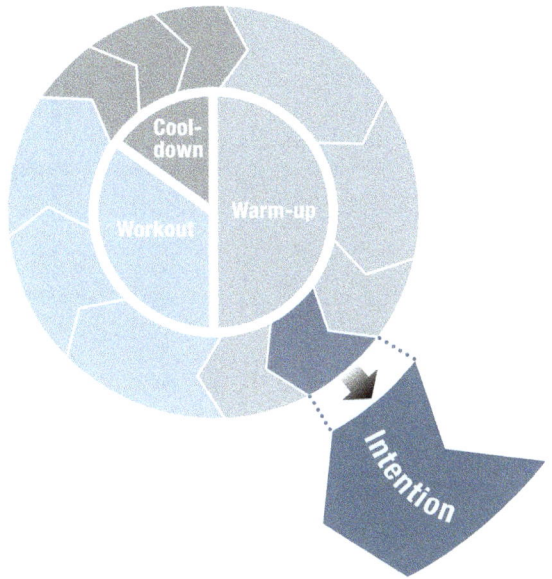

You may recall futurist Zoë Routh's comments about the Future of Feedback in Chapter 1 of this book ('The Future of Feedback', see page 6). She talked about the importance of intention. In 2018, when I conducted my own research, it became evident to me that being clear about the reason feedback is being offered can be highly important to the person receiving the feedback. This was true for all types of feedback, even 'positive' feedback.

Examples of interesting responses to 'positive' feedback include:
- Why are they saying this to me now?
- Why are they sucking up to me?
- What is this really about?
- Is this the start of some sort of 'sh*t sandwich'?

When offering feedback, be explicit about the reason you are offering it *before* you offer it. Put the feedback recipient's mind at ease as soon as possible. Making your intention clear when offering feedback helps to establish trust.

Talking about Intention during the warm-up conversation

The full warm-up conversation is the perfect time to talk about the bigger picture and the reasons you will be offering feedback in the future. Share your general intention with the recipient of your feedback. My own research has found that, when the other person understands the reason(s) why you are offering them feedback, they are usually much more receptive to that feedback.

> ▶▶ *One person's story: An anonymous feedback recipient*
>
> One reaction from someone uncertain of the reason for feedback offered was:
>
> *I'm listening to her feedback, but at the same time I'm wondering, 'Why is she saying this? What is this really about? Is there a hidden agenda here? What's coming next?' It was hard for me to take her feedback seriously because it felt like a bit of a strategic move on her behalf.*

Some examples of how to avoid this feeling of uncertainty in the intended recipients of your feedback are:

- 'Hey Cleo, part of my role as leader is to provide you with useful feedback **because** . . . [stating your general intention in offering feedback to Cleo in the future].'
- 'Hey Cleo, part of my role as leader is to provide you with useful feedback **because** . . .
    - it's important you continue to learn and grow in this role.'
    - it's important you reach your potential.'
    - I want success for you.'
    - it's important you be the best team member you can be.'
    - it's important we provide the best service we can to our clients.'

(or whatever feels and sounds authentic to you . . .)

The magic word

The magic word is 'because'. Using the word 'because' enables you to put the other person's mind at ease. 'Because' sends the message:

There is a reason for the feedback I'm about to offer you. Here is my reason. This is my intention in offering you feedback, you can trust me, I've thought about this, I care about you, I believe in you . . .

Advanced skill: Link your feedback to *their* intentions

Let's keep it real. The other person may not care about *your* intention or *your* reasons for wanting to offer them feedback. After all, it could sound like you are making it about *you*!

One strategy is to turbo charge *your* intentions by referring back to the kind of statements the recipient of your feedback made at the start of the full warm-up conversation when you asked the 'three key questions'. Their answers will have told you:

- what they believe about feedback at work
- what's important to them about feedback at work
- what feedback means to them.

Some people, like Maria (see the conversation below), understand the reason feedback is offered and see that it is intended to benefit them.

▶▶ *A conversation with Maria*

You: 'What's important to you about feedback at work?'

Maria: 'I'd like to think I'm open to feedback. It's a good way to learn and I really enjoy learning.'

You: 'What do you enjoy about learning?'

Maria: 'Oh God, ummm. I guess if I'm learning . . . I think I'm making progress . . . and developing my skills.'

You: 'What's important to you about making progress and developing your skills?'

Maria: 'Well, I'd like to step up into a team leader role one day.'

If, in an earlier warm-up conversation, Maria had shared with you that feedback for her is about making progress, learning and developing her skills because she would like to one day be a team leader, you would be able to link that to what you express to her. The intention behind your feedback could be linked with what she has said is important to her.

Where possible, when doing this, use the feedback recipient's own exact wording:

- 'Hey Maria, part of my role as leader is to provide you with useful feedback because you have shared you are keen to learn and make progress.'
- 'Hey Maria, part of my role as leader is to provide you with useful feedback because further developing your skills is important to you.'
- 'Hey Maria, part of my role as leader is to provide you with useful feedback because you'd like to step into a team leader role one day.'

'Olympic-level' skill: Combine your feedback with mutual intentions

If you feel ready for a super advanced Feedback Offering skill, you might like to combine your intention in offering your feedback with the intention of the person receiving the feedback. This is a great way to show your support, demonstrate your belief in the other person, and establish a common goal to work towards. Remember to use their *exact* words—this is not about paraphrasing. Here is an example:

> *Hey Maria, part of my role as leader is to provide you with useful feedback* **because** *I want success for you* [your intention]. *The reason we will be having feedback conversations is* **because** *it's important to you that you are making progress, learning and developing your skills, and* **because** *you'd like to step up into a team leader role one day* [her intention]. *I'm here to support you to develop the skills to do that.*

3 Permission: An overview

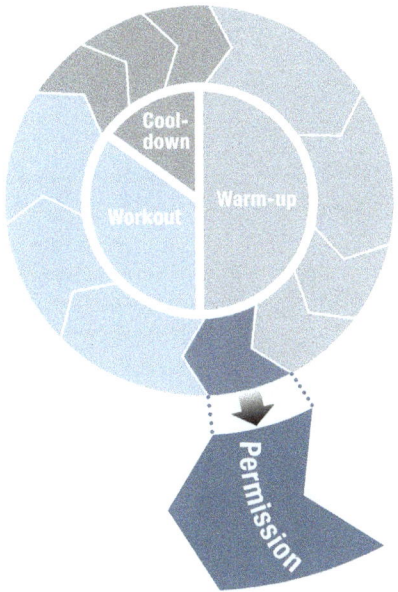

Due to your position as leader, you already have permission to offer feedback within professional relationships. It might seem strange to be asking the person to whom you are offering feedback for permission to do so when you already have it, but this is an approach that works! The benefits include the effects of showing your respect for the other person, letting them know what to expect, and helping them to feel psychologically safe.

Here is an example:

Part of my role as leader is to provide you with feedback for your growth and development. Are you okay with that?

Think of this as setting expectations and preparing the other person for the feedback to follow. Asking permission is about getting the other person's 'buy-in', and it is making sure there are no surprises in your future feedback conversations. At the same time, it also provides a great opportunity to let the other person know that they also have your permission to ask for feedback from you, as well as your permission for them to offer you feedback.

Make it easy for them! Make sure you share your preferred feedback language with them.

Permission: Scope

A full warm-up conversation provides a great opportunity to make it clear which topics are the ones on which you will be offering feedback in the future. For example, as a leader, you have a responsibility to offer team members feedback on their professional performance. It is not appropriate to offer them feedback on their choice of life partner, their political or religious views, or their diet, binge-watching, parenting . . . etc.

> **Tip:**
> Give each other permission to let the other person know if their feedback is believed to be outside the agreed scope. Discuss how you will do this.

Permission: Agree to disagree

The full warm-up conversation also provides a great opportunity to go 'upstream' (see pages 27–8) and talk about guidelines and boundaries so you can have robust conversations about feedback in a way that aligns with your team values. Talk about examples of when either of you may disagree with some or all of the feedback offered. Discuss when that might happen and how you can both continue to communicate in a professional way, with care and compassion. This is a great time to introduce or revisit team or organisation values.

> **Tip:**
> Give each other permission to disagree with the feedback offered in a way that aligns with your team and/or organisation values. Discuss how you will do this.

Permission: Emotions and armour

We are humans, and part of being human is that we experience emotions. The full warm-up conversation provides a perfect opportunity to discuss emotions that might arise from future feedback conversations. Discuss how you both want to feel in future feedback conversations. Talk about how you would like the other person to respond if you become upset. (We explore emotions and armour in more detail in Chapter 15, 'Power'.)

> **Tip:**
> Give each other permission to talk about the emotions you are experiencing during your feedback conversations. Discuss how you will do this.

BRINGING IT ALL TOGETHER

Have a full 90-minute warm-up conversation (including all of its five parts) once or twice a year. This will set up all your future conversations.

Discuss the:

1 Feedback Offering ladder
2 Feedback Receiving ladder
3 '**T**ailored' approach: Ask the other person their feedback preferences and share yours.
4 '**I**ntention' approach: Share what your general intention will be in offering future feedback.
5 '**P**ermission' approach: Including scope, agreeing to disagree, emotions and armours.

Making it fun

▶▶ *One person's story: Torie*

One leader, Torie, shared her concerns about having warm-up conversations with her team. She stated:

> *As a team we have never discussed feedback. I really like the idea of the warm-up conversation where we talk about feedback, without actually offering any, but how can I start talking to my team about feedback without it being awkward and sounding like I'm about to give them negative feedback?*

My response to Torie's question is: 'Make it fun!' or, as stated earlier, 'Make friends with feedback!'

Why encourage your team to talk about feedback in a fun way?

Many people (who are not yet Feedback Fit) perceive feedback as a potential threat. They probably have a lived experience of that being true for them. To many, both the offering and receiving of feedback feels risky and dangerous. Part of the solution is to encourage your team to talk about feedback. It's kind of like Dr Brené Brown's recommended approach to shame (the more you talk about it, the more its power is reduced); and her approach to emotions (labelling the emotion reduces its power):

> ... *naming an experience, doesn't give the experience more power, it gives us the power of understanding and meaning.*[24]

Questions to encourage your team to have fun talking about feedback

Gather your team and use the following fifteen questions to assist you to have a light-hearted conversation about feedback. As leader, you might like to answer first.

1 'How well did you receive feedback as a teenager?'
2 'Have you ever pretended to take on board someone's feedback, knowing very well that you will disregard it as soon as the conversation is over?'
3 'From which famous person (living or passed) would you like to receive feedback?'
4 'What is the most embarrassing feedback you have received, that at the time was hideous and cringe-worthy, but now makes you laugh?'
5 'What is the most beautiful feedback you have ever been offered?'
6 'If you were to put feedback for yourself on your fridge door or bathroom mirror, what would it say?'
7 'What is the funniest feedback you have ever been offered?'

8   'Describe your best feedback receiving moment.'

9   'What is one of your favourite things about receiving feedback?'

10   'When has feedback made you smile?'

11   'If you wrote a best-selling book about feedback, what would the title be?'

12   'What online tool or app about feedback do you think needs to be invented?'

13   'What is one of your favourite feedback conversations?'

14   'What would your closest friend say about how you offer and receive feedback?'

15   'What would your family say about how you offer and receive feedback?'

Peer-to-peer feedback

In most teams, peer-to-peer feedback is not required when it comes to performance, because offering feedback of that kind is considered the role of the leader. Peers offering feedback that is unwelcome can cause angst in the team. In cases where peer-to-peer feedback is required, ensure it is discussed thoroughly in a warm-up conversation with the whole team, and everyone is in agreement regarding permission, scope and intention.

Is your team comfortable offering peer-to-peer feedback?

▶▶ *One person's story: Torie (again)*

Torie (referred to on page 63) conducted a warm-up conversation with her team of twelve. The intention of the conversation was to generate discussion about how the team members could offer and receive feedback from each other (in other words, peer-to-peer feedback).

A discussion, then a spreadsheet!

After using the fifteen suggested questions to encourage her team to have fun and feel more comfortable talking about feedback with each other, Torie asked everyone to share with the team their feedback receiving preferences in relation to peer-to-peer feedback from their team members. She asked, 'How do you like to receive feedback from your peers?' and also asked them to provide examples.

Torie felt the discussion was useful and, straight after the conversation, she emailed the members of her team and asked them to populate a spreadsheet she called a 'Communal page regarding feedback'. She explained that the spreadsheet would be a reference point for all team members to access at any time.

Torie reflected on the team discussion:

> *They were quite specific in what they wanted, which was useful. For example, some people said they would prefer an email only, so they can process it how they want to. Other people said they didn't want any notice and they would rather just be pulled aside as close to the feedback moment as possible. From that discussion we were able to create the spreadsheet and it's a great team resource, a quick reference point for everyone in the team, so they feel more comfortable offering each other feedback.*

Did anything surprise Torie about the responses?

> *In the discussion one person said not to give her positive feedback in front of other people. Not in a team meeting, not in front of anybody. She shared [that] it made her feel awkward, and she just didn't want it. It was good for me to learn as I had been praising her at our team meetings, thinking I was being a good leader.*

■

Torie's actual spreadsheet obviously included the team members' names, but Torie kindly de-identified the information and shared it with me (see following). It's interesting to see the variation in preferences. (Torie also participated in the exercise herself.)

Summary of Torie's team's Feedback Receiving preferences

▸ In person, but make sure we have time to chat by checking my calendar. Happy to just pop into any free room in private; no notice needed.

- In person, with notice, in private, as soon as practicable.
- In private, no notice. Concrete examples with evidence.
- I am too new to feel completely comfortable yet. Please raise it with my team leader, who can raise it with me.
- Straight away, direct and to the point, so I can make changes if I need to.
- No notice requested for feedback. However, in private and in person is appreciated. Please be open to further discussion so I can gain understanding.
- If you have concerns to raise, please send a request for discussion via text or email advising the purpose of the meeting, unless an immediate action response is required. If you have positive feedback, no notice is required.
- Whenever, wherever. I am not bothered.
- In person and in private, no notice required.
- Positive feedback anytime, no notice, one-on-one or very small group. For example, my office space. Not during team meetings. Constructive or non-positive feedback, one-on-one, written, or a confidential discussion preferred.
- In person and in private. No notice required.
- In person and in private with notice.
- No notice required, but preferably in person and in private. I feel awkward hearing positive feedback. I do not like it. Please provide positive feedback by email, as I will become anxious and overthink it.

What do you assume your team would say if asked about the way they would like to receive peer-to-peer feedback?

> **Tip:**
> Rather than assume, ask them!

Word on the Street

Survey question A

I asked people who had experienced feedback conversations in the workplace to provide an answer to the following:

Describe your best feedback experience in the workplace.

The following list summarises how the survey participants responded.

- Really honest on what was working well and where to improve. Not an attack, but constructive areas to improve.
- When positive feedback was given, along with suggestions on how my work could be improved.
- Positive feedback on what I was doing well.
- I was given encouragement by way of my manager saying my report needed a few tweaks. She provided specific feedback on how to structure the sentences and gave examples of other reports to use to base my structure [on]. It turned a challenging task into one I am now really confident completing.
- Feedback with the opportunity to practise a new skill.
- Strengths-based approach. What I was doing well and how I could stretch in that area and build others' capability in that area as well.
- Feedback from my leader recognising the value and importance of my work.
- Peer feedback—at the right time, considered, helpful.
- Acknowledged what I have done well and why it was helpful.
- My manager had weekly meetings with me and provided me with direction and praise each time. If I needed to improve, this was addressed with honesty and kindness.
- When the feedback has been part of an overall conversation focusing on both the good feedback along with the conversation about where there are opportunities to do even better.
- Open discussion after moving through pre-provided guided questions.

- When guidance is given in a compassionate way, people feel it and grow as individuals.
- Manager letting me know what I had done really well and what they valued from my input, but then gave me ideas on how to improve.
- Regularly scheduled meetings which are structured to include where both I and the direct report can provide feedback.
- Positive reinforcement in a private meeting.
- I asked for the feedback and felt that it was open and honest and constructive—it was given with good intent.
- A previous manager would schedule regular (fortnightly) 'catch-ups' and had a structured set-up that included positives she had heard about our work, checking in with where we sat against expectations, and seeking any positive feedback we had for others around our workplace. I really started looking for positives in others.
- The best experience is being able to have a robust and open discussion with my leader about a project that didn't go so well. We discussed the difficulties we both encountered and how we could work together to improve our communication style.
- Expectations were made clear, and we evaluated my performance against them together before planning how to improve.
- Constructive feedback in the moment. Constructive feedback so that you have something to work on.
- Working with a manager who saw every issue as an opportunity to learn, for change or review. It was under this manager I grew the most.
- Formal monthly meetings, open to honest conversations.
- My manager had a meeting with me for my three-month review. They provided concrete examples of where I was doing well and where I needed to improve.
- During my three-month review my manager brought up the expectations and goals that had been set for my role and worked through what I had achieved, or not, in relation to this. It was really great to have such wonderful feedback.
- Was delivered in a calm manner, with clear examples and support for improvement.

- Honest, respectful/objective and timely, provides context.
- An honest and constructive performance review discussing ways to improve with specific goals.
- Being given encouragement and faith/confidence from my leader (believing I could do it when I didn't think I could).
- Planned sessions where evaluation is expected.
- Holistic feedback. What's going well, what's not and workshopping solutions for growth/improvement.
- When it has been timely, and I've had a say in what the feedback is going to be about.
- One manager who was CONSISTENTLY enthusiastic about what I had done and how I could add more value, without making me feel bad.
- Specific, timely, helpful.
- When I felt that the person genuinely was interested and cared about my development, and it has been delivered in a non-judgemental way.
- In my current job, being recognised for an outcome that had been particularly difficult to achieve.
- Feedback focusing on the professional component rather than the personal component.
- Constructive conversation allowed time for discussions and feedback both ways.

Survey question B

I also asked people who had experienced feedback conversations in the workplace to provide an answer to the following:

Describe your worst feedback experience in the workplace.

The following list summarises how the survey participants responded.

- Delivering feedback, both positive and on areas to improve, via a third party.
- Receiving a document of my work with many harsh comments, including very 'nit-picky' comments and no positive feedback. Later feedback then contradicted earlier comments.

- Open criticism.
- Comparing individuals with differing personalities and styles, and mandating a one-size-fits-all approach for leading-teams.
- Feedback that is too ad hoc and limited.
- Being dressed down without any interest in the facts.
- Direct feedback that has only focused on the negative.
- My leader did an unexpected assessment and told me I failed at the role. That was it, no information on how I could improve.
- Being asked to give feedback to one of my reports that has come from someone else.
- Critical feedback in a group setting.
- Not receiving any feedback that is a toolset to improve. Mostly spoken to poorly, no matter how successful the project or team is going.
- In front of people and I felt demoralised.
- The feedback was not directly given by the person who was meant to give it. It came second-hand and it made me feel unworthy of the conversation.
- When no insights or suggestions on how to further improve are provided. When it's just: 'Great'.
- My worst feedback has been more a lack of feedback. In a previous role I had applied for a promotion (of sorts) and did not receive any feedback or indication of how the application process went, or why I was not offered the job. There was very limited opportunity for me to understand how I could've improved. I found the lack of feedback very frustrating and unmotivating to continue in that job.
- Constantly told bad feedback.
- The person made it all about them. When I raised some things I was struggling with, my leader told me that it was my problem, and they would be CEO one day and this conversation didn't matter.
- Not receiving any and hearing from other people that my manager is not happy.
- Silence.
- Blaming; no opportunity for me to respond; blindsided.

FEEDBACK *Fitness*

- My worst job evaluation was when my manager spent the whole time talking about herself. In the end I asked her was she happy with my work.
- Dominating manager with only criticism.
- Large focus on negatives or things I did wrong with no help or guidance on how to do better next time.
- Told me what I was doing wrong and that maybe I should think about other professions as it doesn't seem that I have what it takes.
- Did not get clear points of improvement, was very general.
- The worst has been when I have asked for feedback and was told they didn't have enough time to speak with me and said, 'I'm sure you are doing fine.' They couldn't even work out a time to speak with me about my performance. This made me reluctant to ask them for feedback.
- Was given during the height of another discussion — seemed like it was tit for tat.
- The lack of feedback or when the feedback has no reference to the role being performed.
- When given non-specific feedback, not sure what I needed to change.
- Lacking context — feedback bomb was thrown with no detail or clarity.
- Sarcastic and judgemental.
- Being called into a manager's office, both standing — them distracted (looking out the window/playing with a chair and yelling at me/telling me in a cryptic way what was wrong with me and what I needed to be careful of).
- When I've heard from others what leaders have said, rather than from the leaders themselves.
- From someone who didn't have all the information and gave negative non-constructive feedback.
- When told you are doing something wrong or could do better in front of others.
- Being told everything I'm doing wrong, no good points.

- Humiliation, 'power' approach in front of the group by the manager.
- Critical feedback with no support.
- Public criticism of work that I have been involved in.
- Ego-based, putting me down to feel better about themselves.
- When matters do not remain confidential, and you lose trust.
- Management blaming me for things out of my control but in their control.
- When you feel like it is given, but not quite sure because the person almost talks in circles.
- In previous job, always being told there were other people quite happy to do our roles and that we could be replaced.
- Flustered, anxious leader.
- Rushed, not prepared, and inaccurate information.

7
Introduction to the Workout Conversation

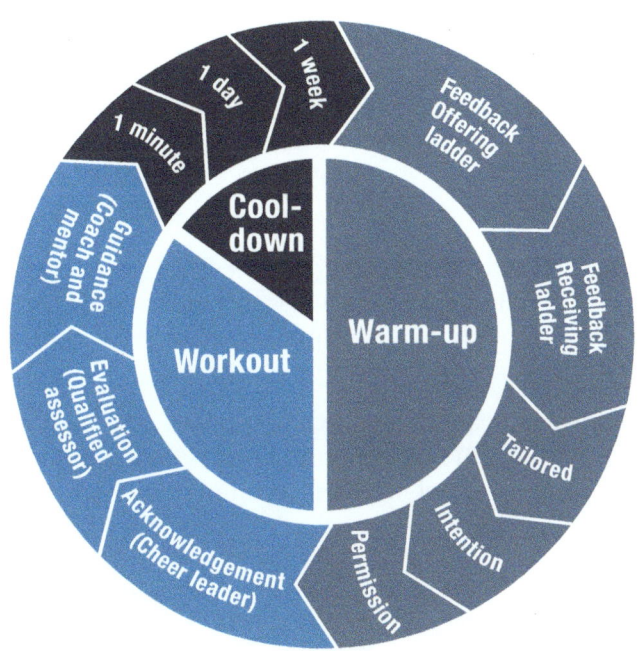

A QUICK REFRESH

The Feedback Fitness framework is made up of three simple steps, the warm-up, the workout, and the cool-down.

Let's have a look at the workout—the juicy, middle step, during which the action happens.

The workout conversation

After the full warm-up conversation has taken place, you will be ready to start having the conversation in which you offer and receive feedback. This second step is called the workout. There might be a degree of sweating and heavy lifting involved. It might feel hard at times but, similar to a physical workout, the endorphins will kick in and you could feel fabulous afterwards!

Allow a period of time to pass between the full warm-up conversation and the next-time conversation, when you actually offer feedback. It is definitely not a good idea to do a full warm-up and then immediately offer feedback. It could feel a bit like a set up on your part—and may feel a bit slimy.

Pre-frame

When you are ready to actually offer feedback, use a pre-frame. A pre-frame is one simple sentence that sets the stage for the feedback you are about to offer. It is one simple sentence that could save you hours of time!

A pre-frame is a great strategy to help prepare the other person for the feedback that will be coming their way. It's a great way to help the other person to feel safe and promote choice, which is very empowering.

JUST TO CLARIFY

Question: Is it best practice to have a full warm-up conversation every time I offer feedback?

Answer: No, once or twice per year is enough.

Question: Is it best practice to use a pre-frame every time I offer feedback?

Answer: Yes! But there are two exceptions:

Exception One: If you are offering feedback on a very regular basis—the pre-frame might start to sound a bit repetitive. (Some alternative options are listed later in this chapter. Use those to mix things up a bit.)

Exception Two: When you are pushed for time and you are offering one-word or two-word 'acknowledgement' ('positive') feedback (such as 'Great', 'Hang in there' or 'Good job'), there is no need to 'prepare' someone for that kind of in-the-moment praise or encouragement.

For everything else, I do recommend a pre-frame. It's a way of showing respect for the other person and building trust between you and them.

A pre-frame is jam-packed full of value!

How to structure your pre-frame

Here is an example:

Hey, Chen. Is it okay if I share something I noticed about the way you interacted with the 'interesting' customer you served before, **because** *I want our customers to rave about our team and I know you want that too.*

The pre-frame in more detail

Here are some things to think about when using a pre-frame.

1. Gain the person's attention by using their name (this is also respectful).
2. Ask permission to offer them feedback.
3. Clearly state the relevant task, skill or behaviour that is the subject of the feedback, and make sure it is something within the person's control.
4. Use the magic word, 'because'.
5. State your specific intention for offering the feedback.
6. Remind the person of the reasons they stated they are open to feedback (from what they shared with you back in the full warm-up conversation).
7. Wait silently for their response. Your role is to bring your observation into their awareness. So give them time to process it and respond.

A dissected pre-frame

The following points dissect the example pre-frame delivered to Chen under the heading 'How to structure your pre-frame' on the previous page, and illustrate how it met the requirements of the seven points also listed on that page.

1. Gain the person's attention by using their name:
   'Hey, Chen . . .'
2. Ask permission to offer the feedback:
   'Is it okay if I share something I noticed about . . .?'
3. Clearly state the relevant task, skill or behaviour:
   '. . . the way you interacted with the "interesting" customer you served before . . .'
4. Use the magic word:
   '. . . because . . .'
5. State your specific intention:
   '. . . I want our customers to rave about our team . . .'
6. Remind them of the reasons they are open to feedback:
   '. . . and I know you want that too . . .'
7. Wait silently. Zip your lips and wait for the response. Then listen to that response when it is offered. Listen, with the aim being to understand, not to argue, correct the other person or defend yourself.

What if the response to your pre-frame is 'No'?

I've been using pre-frames for over sixteen years and, in that time, I've never had anyone respond 'No' to my pre-frame.

I use pre-frames as one way to build rapport and trust. If you and the other person have participated in a full warm-up conversation, I can't foresee any reasons why the other person would say 'No' to your pre-frame—unless something has happened to change things since the warm-up conversation.

Let's say you use the pre-frame, and the other person responds, 'Umm. Actually, no.' It's tempting to ask, 'Why?'—but resist! 'Why?' is not a useful question to ask in this situation. Wherever there is resistance, your role is to build rapport and establish more trust.

Instead of asking 'Why?', increase rapport by asking about the person's wellbeing. Ask them, in your own words, if they are okay. Show care and compassion in your response.

▶▶ *Has something happened outside the workplace?*

Here is a conversation that could take place when something has happened outside the workplace to affect a team member's response:

You: 'Hey, Ned. Can I share something I've noticed about the way you are using the new client management system?

Ned: 'No.'

You: 'Everything okay?'

Ned: 'I've just had a call from the school. They think my son may have broken his arm playing footy. I've got to go pick him up and take him to emergency.'

▶▶ *Has something happened within the workplace?*

Here is a conversation that could take place when something has happened within the workplace to affect a team member's response:

You: 'Hey, Ned. Can I share something I've noticed about the way you are using the new client management system?

Ned: 'No.'

You: 'Everything okay?'

Ned: 'Well, no. [Sounding a little flustered.] I've been trying my best to keep up to date with that system, but it hasn't been letting me input the data properly for the last week. I've contacted IT. It's frustrating. I emailed you about it two days ago, but you haven't responded.'

You: 'Okay I'm here to help. It sounds like you could use some support. Let's talk about how we can sort this out together, so you can feel less frustrated.'

Your pre-frame is a great connecting tool, as long as you are being genuine and authentic. Use the basic structure of the pre-frame examples provided on the previous pages to come up with your own pre-frame wording.

Alternative ways for asking permission in the pre-frame

To prevent the wording of your pre-frames from starting to sound a bit repetitive, some alternative options are listed below.

- 'Is it okay if I share something I have noticed about . . .?'
- 'Can I make an observation about . . .?'
- 'May I share an insight about . . .?'
- 'Can I offer you feedback about . . .?'
- 'Is it okay if I share some information about . . .?'
- 'May I offer another perspective about . . .?'
- 'Is it all right if I offer feedback about . . .'

If you have completed a full warm-up conversation, and a quick one sentence pre-frame, you are ready to offer feedback.

Let's look at three different types of feedback and give you a structure to use for offering them within the workout conversation.

Three types of feedback

TYPE OF FEEDBACK	YOUR ROLE	PURPOSE	EXAMPLE
Acknowledgement feedback	Cheer leader	To motivate	'This is what you are doing well . . .'
Evaluation feedback	Qualified assessor	To evaluate the performance	'This is where you stand in relation to expectations . . .'
Guidance feedback	Coach/mentor	To accelerate the performance	'This is how you can improve . . .'

There are three different types of feedback, recommended to be offered in the following order:

1. 'Acknowledgement' feedback: This is feedback about what someone is doing well.
2. 'Evaluation' feedback: This is feedback about where someone stands in relation to expectations.
3. 'Guidance' feedback: This is feedback about how someone can improve.

Each of the three types of feedback is offered differently and serves a different purpose.

Where possible, offer acknowledgement feedback, followed by evaluation feedback, followed by guidance feedback. The order is super important. Things can go pear-shaped if you skip a step.

To be the most effective leader you can be, work on your skills in providing all three types of feedback.

The three types of feedback will be discussed in detail, separately, in the next three chapters and together in Chapter 11, 'The Three Types of Feedback'.

8
Acknowledgement Feedback

What is acknowledgement feedback?

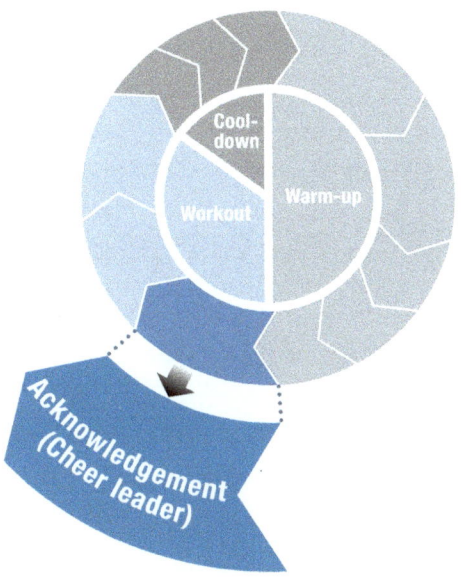

'Acknowledgement' feedback is the description of feedback which shares with another person what they are doing well. You might be tempted to call it 'positive' feedback or praise—however, it is more than just praise.

As well as praising people for their achievements, this kind of feedback can include acknowledgement of the challenging environment in which they are operating (for example, recent fires, floods, restructures, vacancies in their team, change of CEO, etc.). You can also acknowledge factors such as their effort, attitude, progress, output, motivation, growth, patience, dedication, calmness, humour, persistence, and compassion, etc.

Acknowledgement feedback can be used to build rapport and connect with the other person. Use this type of feedback to show your support. It enables you to encourage a team member to keep going when things are tough—and it's the type of feedback that enables you to show support and be there with them, especially if they are underperforming, making mistakes or doubting themselves. It's a chance to show empathy, and to show that you believe in members of your team; and that you care about them and want them to succeed.

Step into the role of 'cheer leader'

For you to offer acknowledgement feedback, it is useful to take on the role of 'cheer leader'. You are more likely to be able to recognise and celebrate what the other person is doing well when you take on that role.

For some leaders, the role of cheer leader comes easily and they love it! When those leaders are cheer leading, they feel good, the other person feels good, and they all feel good together. But that is not true for everyone. I was delivering a Feedback Fitness workshop a few years ago and one leader, shared the following with the group:

> *For God's sake! Do we have to have a morning tea to celebrate people doing their job now do we? I don't praise my team. If they don't hear from me, they know they are doing okay.*

But, do they?

Purpose

The purpose of acknowledgement feedback is to help another person recognise, value and celebrate their progress, persistence and performance. It's a chance to celebrate incremental progress over time. When someone is new, or new to a skill, 'marinate' them in acknowledgement feedback. It helps them feel supported, connected and safe.

Acknowledgement feedback also:
- motivates
- builds relationship
- shows that you care
- inspires
- increases confidence
- reassures.

How to offer acknowledgement feedback

Offering acknowledgement feedback could be as simple as saying, 'Good job on the XYZ task,' as you walk past someone's desk; or making a quick 'Great work' . . . 'Nice' . . . 'You smashed it,' remark just before you start an online meeting. Offering simple acknowledgement feedback can be especially meaningful to people who are worried about underperforming. Reassure them.

You don't need to use a pre-frame before offering simple acknowledgement feedback. Quick, succinct acknowledgement feedback has its time and place, as long as it is not the only way in which you provide that kind of feedback.

The following are some examples of acknowledgement feedback:
- 'Thank you.'
- 'You are going really well.'
- 'I have noticed your effort/focus/contribution/hard work.'
- 'I saw the way you stayed calm under their questioning.'
- 'Your ability to keep on top of the details is amazing.'
- 'I know how hard you have been working and dealing with the challenges of this workplace/situation/environment/current climate, etc.'
- 'Hang in there!'
- 'You have made real progress here.'

Avoid offering 'fluffy' acknowledgement feedback

Although 'Good job' can be meaningful feedback when offered every now and then, it's too vague and general to be the only acknowledgement feedback you offer. People need to know what specifically was 'good', and in what way it was 'good', so they can take the feedback on board and use it in the future.

Following are eight simple criteria to assist you to avoid offering 'fluffy' feedback.

Check that the feedback you offer is:
- meaningful to the other person (Is it important to them; do they care?)

- detailed and specific, rather than global
- within a context, for example 'When presenting in the executive meetings . . .'
- provided in a timely manner
- actionable and repeatable
- within their control
- feedback they can 'make a movie of in their mind'. (Can they 'picture' your acknowledgement feedback? Can they imagine themselves implementing your feedback in the future? For example 'Step into your authority' is hard feedback to 'make a movie' of!)
- 'clean'—stating only what you see and hear. Ensure your statements are free from your judgement, interpretation or diagnoses. For example, 'I heard you sigh on the three occasions when Michael spoke up in the meeting this morning' is a statement of observable fact—and it's pretty hard to argue with facts. Compare that to, 'You were disrespectful to Michael in the meeting this morning.' That latter feedback contains your own (perhaps mistaken) judgement and interpretation and could be met with, 'No, I wasn't.' (You could certainly talk about actual or potential impact of the other person's behaviour after you have listened to their response.)

> **Tips:**
>
> - Discuss acknowledgement feedback in your full warm-up conversation. Some people feel very uncomfortable being offered this type of feedback in a public setting.
>
> - If the person receiving your feedback is new to the skill or role, offer them regular acknowledgement feedback. If they perceive themselves as an expert, or highly skilled, they may find your acknowledgement feedback condescending. Discuss this during the full warm-up.
>
> - In the full warm-up conversation, explain what acknowledgement feedback is and ask for examples of the type of feedback that would mean the most to the other person.

9
Evaluation Feedback

The purpose of evaluation feedback

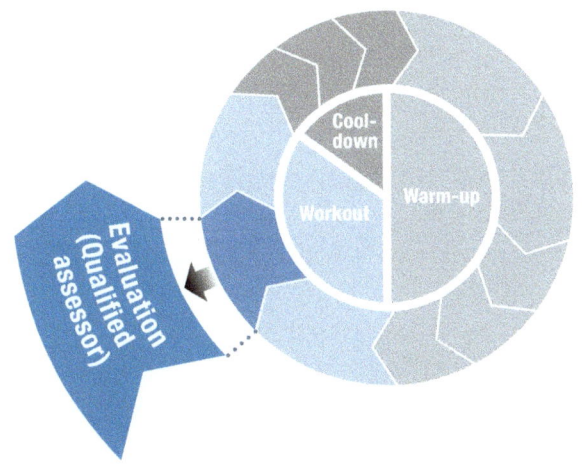

Evaluation feedback is used to let another person know where they stand in relation to expectations. Those expectations could be outlined in their job description, or as key performance indicators in their annual improvement plan. As examples of expectations, you can also use documents such as your team charter, and your organisation's code of conduct or value statements. Make everyone's life easier by using documented expectations and by agreeing, in advance, on the details of how and when these expectations will be measured and reported upon.

Step into the role of 'qualified assessor'

Because you are in a leadership position, you automatically have a level of authority. In other words, you are already qualified to assess another person's performance against agreed predetermined expectations. If you do not believe you are qualified to assess a particular skillset, or your confidence to provide useful evaluation feedback is low in a particular area, it is your responsibility to find someone who can provide useful evaluation feedback.

Step confidently into the role of qualified assessor so you can effectively provide evaluation feedback—and bring your compassion and empathy with you! Supportively, let people know where they stand and ensure that they have the opportunity to adjust accordingly. Show your support and belief in them. Let them know you are there for them. If they choose not to change, that's their decision, but at least you know you have done everything within your power to encourage them to change. They can't claim they didn't know what was needed.

The following points describe the purposes of evaluation feedback and the reasons for offering it.

- It lets the other person know how they are going according to agreed, clear expectations.
- It gives you a chance to talk about the potential impact of another person's performance/behaviour.
- It gives the other person the opportunity to make changes to improve their performance if they choose to (they may not).
- It reassures the other person.
- It provides an opportunity for the other person to ask for help or ask for more challenge.
- It's a chance for you to inform, provide data, and offer a ranking.
- It lets the other person know what they can expect in the future.

How to offer evaluation feedback

Many leaders struggle with evaluation feedback because the expectations are not clear and/or it is unclear how those expectations will be measured. Evaluation feedback involves using an assessment, a rating system, a measurement, or a benchmark (or a carefully considered comparison, when appropriate).

Evaluation feedback is much easier to offer when you have clear expectations and know how those expectations will be measured.

There is no need for interpretation on your part, no judgement, just facts and data. During the full warm-up conversation, discuss, document and clarify expectations, as well as how they will be measured. Make life easier for yourself. No surprises!

As a leader, you are qualified to talk about the impact of behaviour, decisions, attitudes, effort etc. You can offer your evaluation of the impact that team members' actions can have on each other. For example:

- 'I observed you rolling your eyes three times in our team meeting today. According to our team charter, we expect to see zero eye rolling. What I'm concerned about is the impact this could be having on our team culture and how comfortable people feel speaking up in our meetings. Is everything okay?'
- 'I observed you asking Simon for his input three times in our team meeting today. According to our team charter, we want to create a team culture of inclusion and collaboration. The impact of your attempts to encourage Simon appeared to be that he seemed more willing to contribute by the end of the meeting.'
- 'Before our team meeting today, I heard you talking about how much you hate the annual performance review process. What I'm concerned about is the potential impact your comments might have on our two newbies. I will need to catch up with both of them and reassure them of the positives of the process.'
- 'Before our team meeting today, I heard you talking positively about the annual performance review process. The potential impact your comments might have on our two newbies is, hopefully, that they will be open to the process.'
- 'According to your progress to date, your project completion rate is 67%. We need the completion rate to be at least 80% by 30 June for us to secure funding for next year. The impact of this is that the whole team will need to lift to make sure we are hitting our key performance indicators. How can I support you?'
- 'According to your progress to date, your project completion rate is 93%. We need the completion rate to be at least 80% by 30 June for us to secure funding for next year. The impact of already achieving 93% is that the whole team feels more confident we can do it.'

FEEDBACK *Fitness*

Keep your 'but' out of your feedback conversations!

Remember that the order in which the three different types of feedback are offered is important.

1. Acknowledgement feedback: This expresses what is being done well.
2. Evaluation feedback: This expresses how someone is performing in relation to expectations.
3. Guidance feedback: This expresses how someone can improve.

To connect acknowledgement feedback and evaluation feedback, use the word 'and' rather than the word 'but'. 'But' has the power to negate what you have just said! I have seen people's hearts sink when they hear the word 'BUT' straight after receiving acknowledgement feedback. It kind of cancels out the good stuff. It reminds me of those television dating shows: 'You seem like a great guy, BUT . . .'

Compare the following two pieces of feedback.

- 'Hey Jarvis, you are doing A, B and C really well BUT . . .' (in which the 'BUT' is interpreted as: 'but not well enough')
- 'Hey Jarvis, you are doing A, B and C really well AND . . .' (in which the 'AND' is interpreted as: 'let's build on that')!

These examples clearly indicate the difference the use of 'but' and 'and' can make. Remember to start with acknowledgement feedback and then offer evaluation feedback, using the word 'and' to connect the two sentences.

Here are some examples:

- 'You are doing really well at A, B and C, **and** the average number of case closures across the team is four per day. Your average over the last six weeks has been a closure rate of two per day. Let's brainstorm how you can increase your closures.'
- 'You are doing really well at A, B and C, **and** this time last year your sales were this, now they are this—that's an increase of 43%.'

What if the recipient feels upset?

Many leaders worry about the recipient of their feedback getting upset or emotional when offered evaluation feedback—especially if they are not meeting expectations, or they were unaware of the impact of their behaviour on others. This is normal, we are human and part of being human is that we experience emotions. Having a warm-up conversation enables you to talk about emotions and ask how the other person would like you to respond if they become emotional.

When you are offering evaluation feedback, you are in the role of qualified assessor. Although you always aim to treat people with respect and compassion, you still need to state the facts, and this can be confronting for people to hear at times. If you find yourself in this situation, and the other person appears upset about the facts, change your role from qualified assessor back to cheer leader. Amplify your compassion and increase your offer of support.

Remember (from Chapter 8, 'Acknowledgement Feedback'), the cheer leader's role involves more than just praise:

> *Acknowledgement feedback . . . enables you to encourage a team member to keep going when things are tough—and it's the type of feedback that enables you to show support and be there with them, especially if they are underperforming, making mistakes or doubting themselves. It's a chance to show empathy, and to show that you believe in members of your team; and that you care about them and want them to succeed.*
>
> (See page 84.)

If the other person is upset, step into the cheer leader role, empathise and acknowledge their emotions: 'I can see you are upset, is everything okay?' Ask if they would like a break, or would rather continue the conversation. Turn up your listening skills and resist the urge to jump to a solution or attempt to 'fix' their emotions. Rather than pretending there are no tears streaming down the person's face, ask about the tears. 'I can see tears, what's going on for you?' Listen to understand them, not to correct them.

FEEDBACK *Fitness*

Reassure the person you are there to support them to be their best.

Be guided by them as to what they would like to do next. If they decide to end the discussion, let them know this is not the end of the conversation and that you will need to reschedule to discuss the feedback topic.

When you do next discuss the topic, step into the role of cheer leader, then back into the role of qualified assessor. In Chapter 12. 'The Cool-down Conversations', we explore the relevance of cool-down conversations in situations like this.

Tips:
- Provide regular evaluation feedback throughout the year. Don't save it all up! Everyone deserves to be given the opportunity to change.
- Annual performance reviews provide one opportunity for offering and documenting evaluation feedback because they often involve a rating or ranking system: 'According to expectations, this is where you stand.'
- When using ratings or rankings to provide evaluation feedback, use language like: 'You have earned a rating of four.' Rather than: 'I'm giving you a rating of four.'
- ALWAYS offer evaluation feedback *after* acknowledgement feedback, and NEVER on its own.
- Listen to the perspective of the other person *before* you offer any evaluation feedback.
- Keep your 'but' out of feedback conversations, and use 'and' instead.
- Ask about displays of emotion with compassion and empathy.
- Give yourself permission to step back into the cheer leader role if someone becomes upset when you offer them evaluation feedback.

10
Guidance Feedback

What is guidance feedback?

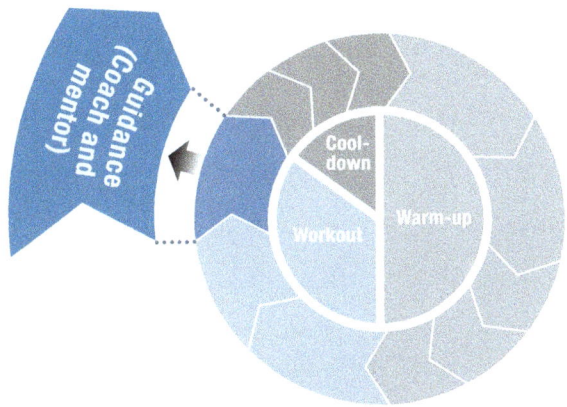

Guidance feedback is about the future. It focuses on ways the recipient of the feedback can improve and it could come in the form of coaching, mentoring, training, teaching or the giving of advice. Its purpose is to help another person to grow and develop their skills and confidence.

It's important that both the person offering the feedback and the person offered the feedback have a 'growth mindset'. (You might like to check out the work of Professor Carol Dweck regarding the importance of having a growth mindset when it comes to offering and receiving feedback.[25] To summarise her approach, Dweck believes that it is possibly more important to adopt a mindset encouraging growth and receptivity to learning than to just have innate potential.)

Step into the role of coach and mentor

When offering guidance feedback, step into the role of coach, mentor, trainer, teacher, presenter, facilitator, author, speaker, etc. Guidance feedback involves any role in which you share your knowledge and experience, or ask powerful questions. Many leaders love this role; they love seeing their team members grow and develop.

What is the purpose of guidance feedback?

Guidance feedback provides the person receiving it with the opportunity to learn, change and grow by identifying and outlining their next steps. Many of my coaching clients have shared how they love growing and learning in their role. Some have said, 'If I'm not learning in the role, I will leave.'

Use guidance feedback to keep your team members engaged.

The benefits of guidance feedback

The list below summarises common benefits resulting from guidance feedback delivered well.

Guidance feedback:
- helps its recipient to adapt, pivot, learn and grow
- increases professional growth
- helps its recipient to improve performance
- accelerates learning
- inspires its recipient to step into thinking about future possibilities
- helps identify a person's possible next steps.

How to offer guidance feedback

Give yourself permission to fully step into the role of coach and mentor. Turn up your continuous improvement thinking and respectfully share your knowledge with the other person. If you use more of a coaching approach to your leadership, ask powerful questions rather than just tell (that will be the subject of the next book I'm writing).

Back yourself. You have knowledge, expertise, insight and wisdom to share. Show the other person you believe they can grow and learn. Inspire them to strive for greatness.

Guidance feedback is about the future. It is a great opportunity to ask the other person to collaborate with you regarding improvements:

> *Okay, this is what happened last week. What can we do next time? What's something we can brainstorm and go through? What might it look like next time this happens?*

The following are some examples showing how guidance feedback can be delivered:

- '... *and*, for you to take your performance to the next level, you might like to ...'
- '... *and* have you considered ...?'
- '... *and*, for you to improve, a possible next step is ...'
- '... *and*, to keep the momentum going, lets plan for ...'
- '... *and* a great learning focus could be to ...'
- '... *and*, for you to increase your expertise in XYZ, you might like to...'
- '... *and* what do you think you could do differently next time?'

> **Tips:**
> - Guidance feedback is best offered after acknowledgement feedback and evaluation feedback have both been offered.
> - If you are offering feedback to an 'interesting' person (at the bottom of the Feedback Receiving ladder), avoid telling them what to do. Avoid saying: 'You should/have to/need to/must.' But, if there is ever serious risk, of course you are authorised to tell/direct/instruct them.
> - When offering feedback to someone at the bottom of the Feedback Receiving ladder, use language such as, 'You might like to ...', 'You may not agree with this ...', or 'Colin from accounts had a similar issue and he figured it out by ...'.

11
The Three Types of Feedback

Each of the three types of feedback is offered differently and serves a different purpose. All three types of feedback play a part.

BRINGING IT ALL TOGETHER

Here is an example of a feedback conversation which models the offering of feedback as it has been described on the previous pages:

You: 'Hey Iris, can I offer you feedback about some skills/tasks/behaviour, because I know you like to grow and learn in your role?'

Iris: 'Sure.'

You: 'What I'm noticing is your commitment to the team in the way you speak up and share your ideas in meetings and, for someone who has been in this role for six months, we would expect your performance to be here; you are currently here, and for you to take your performance to the next level, you might like to do X, Y and Z.'

This approach to the offering of feedback fulfils all the necessary stages and content outlined earlier in the following ways.

The pre-frame:

Hey Iris, can I offer you feedback about some skills/tasks/behaviour, because I know you like to grow and learn in your role?

Acknowledgement feedback:

What I'm noticing is your commitment to the team in the way you speak up and share your ideas in meetings . . .

Evaluation feedback:

... and, for someone who has been in this role for six months, we would expect your performance to be here, you are currently here ...

Guidance feedback:

... and for you to take your performance to the next level, you might like to do X, Y and Z.

▶▶ One person's story: Sarah

This story shows the importance of offering three different types of feedback.

Of the three types of feedback, Sarah, like many leaders, was comfortable providing team member Jeremy with acknowledgement feedback and guidance feedback. She thought she was doing a great job at providing feedback and was annoyed with Jeremy, who seemed to ignore the valuable feedback she offered him.

In our coaching session, Jeremy came to realise that he hadn't been clear with Sarah about the *type* of feedback he was seeking from her. He was wanting information regarding how she thought he was going in his role, because he knew of an upcoming opportunity to become a team leader and wanted to know where he stood so he could decide whether it was worth him applying for it. He wanted evaluation feedback but, instead, he was frustrated as a result of receiving acknowledgement feedback and guidance feedback.

Some leaders offer acknowledgement feedback and guidance feedback on a regular basis—but not evaluation feedback. Then they drop an evaluation feedback bomb in an annual performance review—with no warning or warm-up. The person who receives it is shocked by the sudden evaluation feedback, especially if the feedback indicates that their performance is not meeting the agreed (possibly unclear) expectations of the role and this is the first time they have heard it.

▶▶ *My story: What I learned delivering a workshop*

Recently I was delivering a Feedback Fitness workshop to a team of leaders. I asked them:

> Which type of feedback do you feel the most confident in offering?

I put up three different posters around the room and asked the leaders to vote with their feet.

About 60% of the leaders walked to the 'acknowledgement feedback' poster (indicating they selected that), and the remaining leaders walked to the 'guidance feedback' poster. No one—not *one single* leader—walked to the 'evaluation feedback' poster.

Why was that?

Many leaders are not sure how to provide evaluation feedback. They worry about mucking it up, and the consequences of that, so they avoid it. They anxiously begin the workout conversation with no warm-up and, possibly, not much transparency or trust. It doesn't feel psychologically safe for either party.

As one leader explained:

> *I understand the idea of the three different types of feedback. I'm okay with evaluation feedback when [people] are meeting or exceeding the expectations. It's when they are not meeting expectations that I don't know what to say. I worry I will say the wrong thing and demoralise them.*

Make friends with evaluation feedback

Talk about evaluation feedback in the full warm-up conversation. Ask the other person about their 'It depends' responses in regard to evaluation feedback. Talk with them about what the best approach to having a conversation would be if they were not meeting expectations in the future. Ask them what they find most useful about evaluation feedback.

My experience is that most people would rather know sooner rather than later if they are not meeting expectations. The person being offered your feedback deserves an opportunity to improve with your guidance and other support. As Dr Brené Brown says, 'Clear is kind. Unclear is unkind.'[26]

Just like elite athletes who improve by doing the preparation, laying the groundwork, and practising, you can become 'world-class' at offering evaluation feedback by using the same approach.

BRINGING IT TOGETHER

As you reflect on your leadership, if you had been one of the leaders in the workshop decribed on the previous page, which poster would you have walked to? What would it take for you to feel confident in offering *all three* types of feedback?

Word on the Street

Survey question

I surveyed 93 local government leaders, and asked:

> In which role do you feel most confident when offering feedback?

The results are shown in the diagram below:

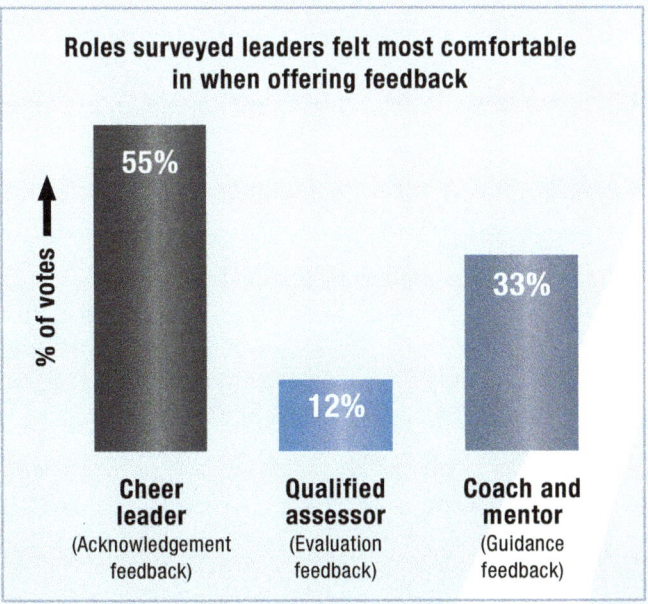

The majority of the leaders surveyed were most confident when offering acknowledgement feedback (55%), and least confident when offering evaluation feedback (12%). No wonder (based on this data) that many leaders dread annual performance reviews! They don't feel as confident as they would like to feel when offering evaluation feedback.

Offering feedback online: 'Yes' or 'No'?

For some organisations, feedback conversations have been happening online successfully for many years. Think of an organisation with team members located in various places around the globe. Online communication, including the offering of feedback, is normal practice for them. For others whose idea of best practice is to offer feedback face-to-face, COVID created a new challenge—whether to have feedback conversations online, or wait until both parties were back 'in the office'?

When I was coaching leaders during COVID, many of those leaders were based in Melbourne, Australia, the most locked-down city in the world. Some leaders shared with me that they kept putting off feedback conversations until:

> ... we are back in the office so we can have it face-to-face.

Unfortunately, that often meant waiting months on end for restrictions to be lifted—so some feedback conversations, especially more challenging ones, never happened. After lockdowns ended, many leaders were busy trying to reconnect with their team members and build trust with them, and they were not going to risk damaging those relationships with feedback conversations—that was just too risky!

The first part of the solution to this issue can be found in Chapter 4, 'Introduction to the Warm-up Conversation' (which explores the conversations you have about feedback before you offer or receive any feedback). During the warm-up conversation raise the subject of the possibility of feedback being offered online. That way there will be no surprises, and no unspoken expectations about feedback conversations only occurring face-to-face. The warm-up conversation provides a great opportunity to hear any concerns or worries the other person might have about feedback conversations occurring online—and also provides a chance to work through those concerns.

Here is an example of an approach that could be taken when raising the subject of online feedback during a full warm-up conversation:

Hey Tahira, as discussed so far, we are going to be having regular feedback conversations. Due to our hybrid working arrangements, some of these may happen face-to-face and, at other times, online or even over the phone. Of course, some of our cool-down conversations could also happen online.

Just to be clear, when we have feedback conversations online, I will follow up with you later that day or the next day and then, about a week later, we will revisit the feedback.

Have you any thoughts on that? How do you feel about that? Do you have any concerns about us having these conversations online?'

The second part of the solution in regard to offering feedback online can be found in Chapter 12, 'The Cool-down Conversations', in which the importance of cool-down conversations is discussed. The cool-down is the name I give to the series of conversations occurring after you have offered feedback. It's about what happens immediately after you have offered the feedback, and also when you follow up the next day, and about a week later.

When you offer feedback and are in the same room as the person to whom the feedback is being offered, you are most likely to see the person again soon after that feedback conversation. You might be in another meeting with them, or see them at their desk, or bump into them in the lift or at the coffee shop.

When you are in the same physical location, you are able to: check out their body language; notice if they left the feedback conversation and went directly to the manager of HR; or notice if they came back into the office space and sat at their computer silently for the next three hours. When you have offered feedback online, once you hit 'Leave Meeting', the person who received your feedback disappears from your view. You can't read their body language, or see, or hear them. That means it is a lot harder to check on their wellbeing.

What Dr Libby Brook says

Organisational psychologist and expert in psychological health and safety Libby Brook has said the following about the offering of feedback online:

> *The challenge is around whether or not you can predict what environment they're going to be in; whether or not they have other demands or current distractions that are going to interrupt the conversation. When you finish the online conversation, you end the meeting, and you are not there in the same space as them. This can be problematic in some ways because it means that you could then avoid each other. That could potentially be challenging for the maintenance of that relationship because it becomes quite a distinct 'feedback' conversation rather than just a continuation of your relationship. What can be missing are some of those relationship-building social cues or social moments which can normalise the feedback conversation and give some perspective.*[27]

The solution to this issue is to ensure you conduct cool-down conversations after you offer feedback online. Those cool-down conversations can happen online! We explore that in Chapter 12, 'The Cool-down Conversations'.

Word on the Street

> **Survey question**

This question was asked of people who had received all three types of feedback:

> What do you believe about the three different types of feedback?

The following list summarises how the survey participants responded.

- It was useful when positive feedback was given along with suggestions on how my work could be improved.
- A previous manager would schedule regular (fortnightly) 'catch-ups' and had a structured set up that included positives she had heard about our work, checking in with where we sat against expectations, and seeking any positive feedback we had for others around our workplace.
- Expectations were made clear, and we evaluated my performance against them together before planning how to improve.
- I appreciated being told in a clear way my areas of improvement.
- Acknowledgement of what I was doing well then followed up with areas I can continue to work on to become a better clinician.
- My manager had a meeting with me for my three-month review. They provided concrete examples of where I was doing well and where I need to improve. In both cases, reasons . . . why were provided and, when speaking about improving, I was given direction about how to improve.
- Open, honest discussion explaining what I'm doing well, followed by the benefits [to me and others] of [me] improving in certain areas . . . and asking how I think I might do this, followed by a discussion on how to get there.
- Just giving positive feedback all the time without any constructive feedback can also be damaging and unhelpful.

12

The Cool-down Conversations

The purpose of cool-down conversations

Don't rely on courage alone

You have had the courage to offer feedback, now let's make sure you get the best return on that investment. If the conversation goes pear-shaped, you need to have a system already in place to fall back on, so you are not relying on your courage alone.

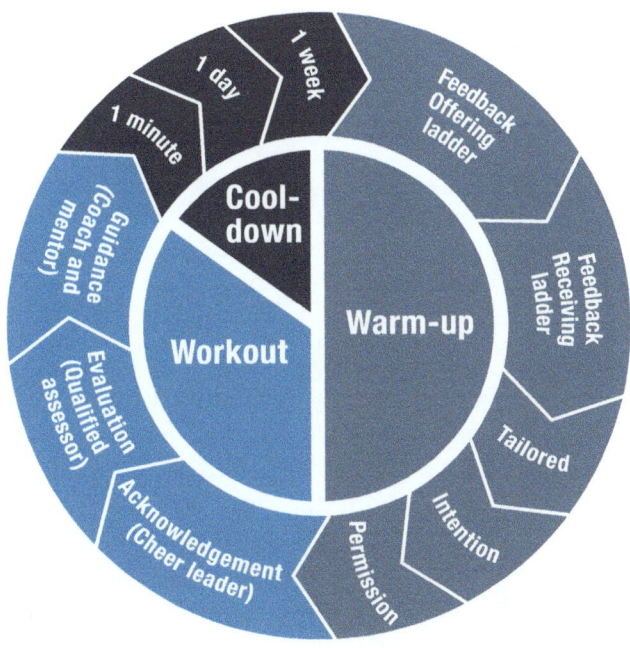

A cool-down conversation is the responsibility of the person who offered the feedback.

The purpose of cool-down conversations is to check on the wellbeing of the person who has received the feedback, ensure that your relationship with them has been not been negatively affected, and to check on the effectiveness of the feedback itself.

These conversations provide the other person with the opportunity to ask for further clarification. Don't leave people wondering what your feedback meant. Think of this as a review of the effectiveness and impact of the workout conversation.

Are you 'circling back' in your feedback conversations?

What Dr Brené Brown says

Dr Brené Brown uses the term 'circling back' to describe the revisiting of a feedback conversation after she has had time to think about the feedback offered to her.

In her book *Dare to Lead: Brave work. Tough conversations. Whole hearts*, Brown describes a time when she received feedback from her team:

> After listening, I thanked them for their courage and honesty and promised again that I would think about it. I asked if we could **circle back** the next day.[28]

In this situation, Brown is talking about 'circling back' *after* she had been offered feedback. My own observation is that many people being offered feedback are reluctant to ask the person who offered the feedback to circle back, particularly if they have felt uncomfortable when receiving the feedback. They often want to escape and will say anything to rush though a hard conversation so it can be over—with almost a 'Get me out of here' response! They also might then actively avoid the person who offered them the feedback. Given that, it is obviously important that the person offering the feedback does circle back, especially if they are a leader and the feedback has been offered to someone they lead.

What does circling back involve?

Circling back on feedback conversations involves revisiting and keeping the conversation going. It gives you, as a leader, the opportunity to:

- **care and support:** Meaning checking in on the other person, showing you care and answering any questions they have. This is especially important if you have offered your feedback online.
- **learn and grow:** Which means to explore what you can both learn from the feedback conversation and the implementation (or not) of the offered feedback.
- **celebrate, or plan for the future:** This refers to the chance that circling back provides for valuing and acknowledging growth, progress and skill development; and to apply a continuous improvement approach to the next steps.

How to circle back in your feedback conversations

The third step of the Feedback Fitness framework actively encourages circling back. In fact, that cool-down phase is all about circling back.

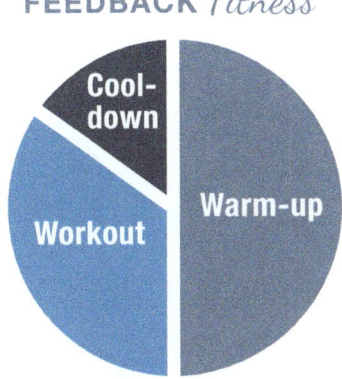

FEEDBACK *Fitness*

The cool-down is made up of three simple conversations, which are simple to use—and super easy to remember.

The three conversations take place:
- one minute after the workout conversation
- one day after the workout conversation
- one week after the workout conversation.

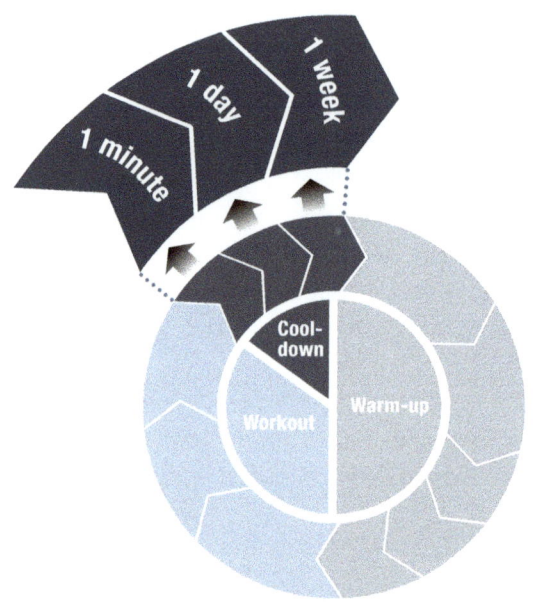

An explanation of the timing of cool-down conversations

One minute after the workout conversation

Immediately after the workout conversation (when you have just offered the feedback), check on the other person's wellbeing. This might not always be practical because you might be interrupted, or they might need to rush off to their next back-to-back meeting. But still check on their emotional state as soon as you can. Ask them how they are feeling about the feedback. Think of it as checking in on their emotional safety.

Is there anything they need to do to regulate their emotions?

One day after the workout conversation

The purpose of the 'one day later' conversation is to check in after the recipient of your feedback has had a chance to process and reflect on the feedback offered to them. Keep in mind, if there was little or no warm-up conversation prior to the feedback being offered, people may experience a stress-response to feedback. As a result of their emotional response to it, they might be less able to process the feedback being offered to them, let alone remember it the next day.

This cool-down conversation could occur later the same day as the feedback was offered, on the next day, or even two days later. The point is that you are checking in on the relationship you have with the person who received your feedback, which is important because the number-one concern for many people is that offering feedback will damage their relationship with the other person. Importantly, by following up a day or two later you are providing the other person with an opportunity to ask clarification questions, and are providing yourself with an opportunity to offer support.

If you offered the feedback online, your cool-down conversations can also all occur online.

The 'one day later' cooldown conversation provides an opportunity for you to ask what meaning the recipient of your feedback has given to that feedback. In Chapter 15, 'Power', you will read about PhD student Chloe who, on receiving a lot of feedback from her supervisor, initially interpreted his feedback as, 'He thinks I am dumb', but later changed that interpretation to the more useful: 'He is doing his job and I'm learning.' (See page 138.)

One week after the workout conversation

This conversation is intended to be carried out one week—approximately—after the feedback was offered and received. You could have the conversation earlier if you know it was possible for the feedback to be implemented earlier. Or the conversation might not happen until two weeks later to allow enough time for the feedback to have been implemented.

The purpose of this third cool-down conversation is:
- to determine whether the feedback has been implemented, and to what degree
- to gauge the impact of the implementation
- to celebrate progress, courage, learnings, effort, wins ...
- to discuss and plan next steps
- to discuss the usefulness of the feedback you offered
- for you to ask for feedback on your feedback offering skills!

> **Tip:**
> A great 'go to' question you might like to use in the 'one week later' conversation is, 'What was most useful for you about the feedback?'

Considerations:
- how you can set up a system to ensure you are scheduling 'cool-downs' after you offer feedback to others
- how cool-down conversations have been useful in the past
- whether you have created a team culture in which cool-down conversations are normal, expected and encouraged.

Keeping the feedback conversation going

When leaders use the language 'giving feedback', it often sounds like it is describing a one-off 'event', rather than a series of conversations. Feedback happens within interactions—with conversations occurring within a relationship, and in a shared context and environment. The danger of adopting the 'event' approach, rather than the conversation approach, is that it can feel awkward (for both parties) to keep the conversation going once the feedback has been offered.

The 'one week later' cool-down conversation can be used to keep the feedback conversation going.

The following diagram shows the different scenarios that can follow from the offering of feedback.

The Cool-down Conversations

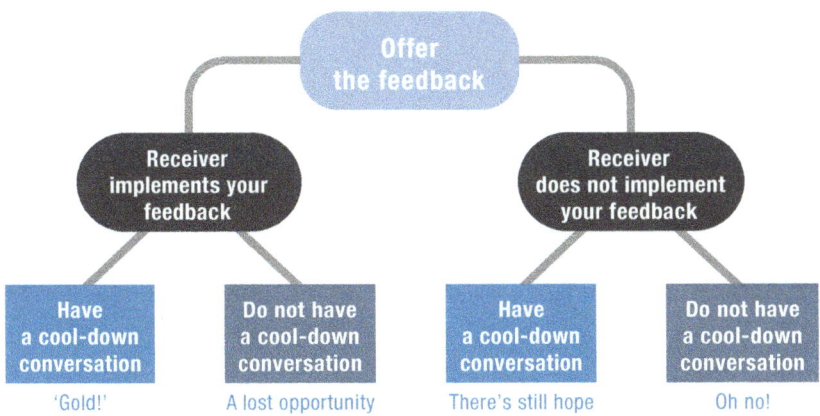

Scenario 1: Gold!
(Implementation AND a 'one week later' cool-down conversation)

This is the best scenario! You offer the feedback during the workout conversation, it is implemented, and then you have a cool-down conversation about the impact of the implementation and what worked well, including discussion and planning of the next steps. The feedback conversation continues. This is good!

Scenario 2: A lost opportunity
(Implementation and NO 'one week later' cool-down conversation)

The feedback you offered has been implemented, but there is no further discussion about the impact of the implementation, or about the next steps. The opportunity to build on the implementation is lost. Celebration does not occur, and future changes are not suggested. This might be okay in certain situations, but you will have lost the opportunity to build momentum.

Scenario 3: There's still hope
(No implementation AND a 'one week later' cool-down conversation)

You have offered the feedback, it has not been implemented, so you have a conversation about what got in the way of implementation.

Your role in this conversation is to listen. Listen to the other person's perspective before you talk about next steps and future plans. Offer your support; and make sure the other person has a chance to discuss barriers or obstacles to implementing your feedback. The conversation continues in a productive way. It's not ideal—but there is still hope. At least you have had the courage to continue the conversation.

Scenario 4: Oh no!
(No implementation and NO 'one week later' cool-down conversation)

This is the worst-case scenario. You have offered the feedback, it has not been implemented, and you have not had a conversation about what got in the way of implementation. There has been no discussion of next steps. The situation may feel awkward. Sometimes it can feel like there is an elephant in the room. Leave it too long and it could feel too uncomfortable to mention the topic again.

> **Tip:**
> Remember that the three separate cool-down conversations ('one minute later, 'one day later' and 'one week later') are the responsibility of the person who offered the feedback.

As you can see from what has been discussed earlier in this chapter, you can use the cool-down to ensure feedback conversation continues. As the person offering the feedback, it is your responsibility to initiate the cool-down conversations whether the feedback was implemented or not. Both parties might need to step into a position of courage to keep the conversation going.

Use the cool-down to be accountable

As much as the cool-down conversations are about the psychological safety of the person being offered the feedback, they also provide an opportunity for you to reflect on the way you offered the feedback and to be accountable for your own muck ups.

Be kind to yourself. Sometimes, in the moment, we blurt things out in a way of which we are not proud. (I'm GUILTY as charged!).

The cool-down is a chance to learn from past mistakes, so you can improve your feedback offering skills for next time.

> ••• What Dr Brené Brown says •••
>
> Consider American professor and researcher Brené Brown's thoughts, expressed when she was discussing the offering of feedback:
>
> *I think sometimes you earn more trust if you screw it up and circle back than if you would have done it really well. . . I'll say stuff like, 'You know, when you replied this way, I said this and I saw something shift in you; I felt like the space between us went from open and curious together to weird, and I just want to check in.*[29]

Are three cool-down conversations necessary?

You might be asking: 'Do I seriously need to have three cool-down conversations every time I offer feedback?'

The answer is 'No'.

Back yourself to use your own judgement on this. If you have a great full warm-up conversation, there will be times when you offer feedback and then decide there is no need to have a cool-down conversation.

If you are not sure how the other person is feeling about your feedback, or they are perceived to be on a rung towards the bottom of the Feedback Receiving ladder, think of the cool-down conversation as like taking out insurance. Speaking from my own awkward feedback offering experiences, you can't assume people don't need to do a cool-down just because you think the workout conversation went well.

13
Receiving Feedback

When I'm receiving feedback, and I want to stay aligned with my value of courage, I say to myself, 'I'm brave enough to listen.'[30]

Dr Brené Brown

The Feedback Receiving formula

Now that you have the information to become skilled in offering feedback, how skilled are you at receiving it? The Feedback Receiving formula provides you with the tools and strategies to be able to choose how you respond to even the most 'interesting' feedback offered to you. With this formula, you will be more empowered to choose what you think about the feedback, choose how you feel about the feedback, and choose not to take feedback personally.

The Feedback Receiving formula is made up of three ingredients:

1. mindset
2. power
3. esteem.

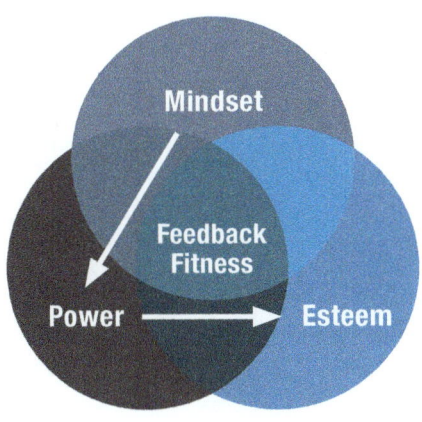

Mindset

When it comes to receiving feedback, your mindset is your most powerful tool. Your beliefs and thinking styles have a huge impact on how you experience feedback. You are able to choose what you make the feedback offered to you mean.

Power

You have four personal powers which allow you choice in how you respond to feedback offered to you.[31] When responding to feedback, you have choice in what you:

1. believe
2. feel
3. say
4. do.

Use these four powers to empower yourself in feedback conversations.

Esteem

There are different ways of thinking in regard to confidence and esteem. How you think about confidence and esteem impacts your openness to feedback. You can reach a point at which feedback does not positively or negatively affect how you feel about yourself.

The Feedback Receiving self-assessment

To be Feedback Fit means practising all three parts of the formula (mindset, power and esteem). It's kind of like a triathlon; you will be best at receiving feedback when you are strong in all three components. Similarly to competing in triathlons, the more you practise, the better the results you will achieve.

The following diagram was introduced in Chapter 5, 'Feedback Self-assessments' (see page 46), along with an itemised description of the characteristics of people who place themselves on different rungs of this Feedback Receiving ladder. Refer back to that if you need to.

How you feel when receiving feedback	Openness to receiving feedback
Resilient	80–99%
Receptive	60–80%
Reluctant	40–60%
Resistant	20–40%
Rejecting	0–20%

As was described in Chapter 5, 'Feedback self-assessments', people can be encouraged to 'make friends with receiving feedback' (see pages 42–5). Fifty questions were provided to be used in warm-up conversations to encourage members of your team to reflect on and share their own beliefs about *receiving* feedback.

Asking for feedback

It takes courage for someone to ask for feedback, especially if they are unsure of what the response will be. Keep in mind that, for many people, it also takes courage to offer feedback when asked to do so (think back to the Feedback Offering ladder on page 36).

Here is a handy checklist for reference when asking for feedback:

▶ Revisit your list of 'It depends' responses regarding receiving feedback.
▶ Ensure the person you are asking for feedback is qualified to provide useful feedback.
▶ Discuss the confidentiality of the feedback conversation.
▶ Ask if the person is comfortable and willing to offer you feedback.
▶ Ask for feedback in regard to skills, roles, behaviours, but not about you as a person.
▶ Ask for feedback on specific topics, rather than 'general' feedback.
▶ Describe to the person the scope and context of the feedback you would like.

- Explain the intention you have in asking for the feedback.
- Explain what you are planning to do with the feedback.
- Allow the person to decide when and how they will provide the feedback.
- Ask for all three types of feedback—acknowledgement feedback, evaluation feedback and guidance feedback.
- Give the person time to prepare—most people want to provide you with high quality feedback which does take time and thought.
- Thank the person for the feedback, even if it proves to be a 'growth opportunity'.
- Ask for a cool-down conversation, in which you can circle back to them for clarification, or to let them know you have implemented the feedback they offered you.

Word on the Street

Survey question

I asked people:

> What do you believe are the barriers to people receiving feedback in their workplace?

I have sorted the responses into the six main categories to which they referred:

1. The receiver
2. The person offering the feedback
3. Emotions
4. Time constraints
5. Relationships
6. Systems and culture.

1 The receiver

The following list summarises how the survey participants responded.

- Most direct reports are reluctant to receive feedback—they are already closed off.
- They are not used to receiving any constructive feedback.
- Not wanting to hear the feedback and getting defensive.
- Lack of accountability.
- Poor listening and understanding of the feedback.
- Resentment of supervisor; resistance to learning.
- High egos and thinking they don't need guidance.
- They disagree with the feedback. Complain to other staff members about how they have been treated or wronged. Not willing to change or step up.
- Reluctance to change.
- Unless it is good feedback, people do not want to hear evaluation feedback and guidance feedback.
- Lack of self-awareness.
- Limited knowledge on how to receive feedback.
- Not wanting to take responsibility for their behaviour.
- Their own ego.
- Belief that they do enough already.
- People aren't receptive to feedback.
- Not seeing the benefits of getting feedback.
- People disagreeing with or not accepting the feedback.

2 The person offering the feedback

The following list summarises how the survey participants responded.

- Lack of leadership training.
- Poor feedback style and method.
- It is often poorly delivered.
- It is not meaningful or actionable.

- Lack of appreciation for work done.
- Not offered in a timely manner and it comes as a surprise.
- Poor communication: timing of feedback—it is often after the fact, can be a good learning outcome, but is often too late for the necessary situation.
- Lack of clarity in feedback offered.
- Inconsistent goals, expectations and lack of clear supported leadership.
- Lack of expectations.
- Unaware of expectations.
- Poor expectations.

3 Emotions

The following list summarises how the survey participants responded.

- Feeling like they are being criticised.
- Poorly offered feedback in the past.
- Taking it personally. Hear it as criticism, not as an opportunity to learn.
- Feeling criticised.
- People's personal feelings about how to receive feedback.
- Taking feedback at a personal level.
- Too sensitive.
- Fear of feeling criticised/not good enough.
- Lack of courage.
- Constantly feeling judged by the community—don't need it from your supervisor as well.
- Sensitivity and defensiveness.
- Feeling negative about your abilities.
- They are scared they aren't doing well.
- People taking feedback personally; managers not being confident in giving feedback.

- The fear of receiving feedback that isn't necessarily on the positive side.
- People taking things personally.
- Lack of self-esteem.
- Lack of ability of those receiving feedback to do so comfortably and not become defensive.
- Take it personally/emotional; workplace stress.
- Pride.
- Fear of not being good enough.
- Negative feelings associated with feedback—society-ingrained expectations about what feedback means.
- Not feeling comfortable enough with the leadership team.
- May induce fear.
- Feeling under threat or stress already—so it's harder not to get defensive.
- People take the matters as a personal attack rather than seeing it as an improvement to process.
- Fear or reluctance to hear negative feedback.

4 Time constraints

The following list summarises how the survey participants responded.
- Being too busy.
- Time constraints 'x 4'.
- Finding time to put aside to talk to people.
- Having an appropriate time and place to provide the feedback.
- Enough time for meetings to occur for this feedback to be given.
- Not having the time available.
- Time with my direct manager.
- Due to the 'tyranny of the urgent' mindset in our workplace, feedback is often only given priority when it is used as a warning for behaviour, leading a lot of staff to hate 'feedback'.
- Lacking time to guide and coach, then review.

5 Relationships

The following list summarises how the survey participants responded.

- Misunderstanding or misinterpretation, relationships and motivation levels.
- Lack of trust in the motivation of the leaders.
- Prior negative experience in receiving feedback.
- Lack of getting to know new bosses.
- Power dynamics between management and workers.
- In some cases, there is a lack of trust between the employee and the manager.
- Building relationships with leadership and respect; leaders who walk the talk.
- Poor relationships.
- Distrust.
- Lack of communication; leadership not getting to know staff.
- How will the other person take it? Will they personalise it or not?

6 Systems and culture

The following list summarises how the survey participants responded.

- A lack of psychological safety.
- Lack of processes implemented.
- It's not part of the culture.
- Cultural practice—constructive feedback is seen as negative or even performance management.
- Performance management is not being addressed in the business and employees believe they are doing a good job as a result. When we then attempt to provide constructive feedback, they take it personally.
- Ineffective performance review process.
- It has not been usual practice.
- Never seeing good role models of receiving feedback.

14

Mindset

Beliefs about feedback

How a person thinks about receiving feedback supports their feedback receiving behaviour and holds it in place. If they believe that receiving feedback is dangerous, a threat or something to avoid, that thinking will result in them trying to avoid feedback—and they certainly will not be seeking it out.

Let's carry out a quality check on the usefulness of beliefs about receiving feedback. Listed below are some of the common beliefs expressed.

Limiting beliefs

- Feedback makes me feel awful about myself.
- Feedback means I'm not good enough.
- Feedback means I've done something wrong.
- Feedback means I'm in trouble.
- People use feedback as a way of belittling me.
- I take feedback personally.

Useful beliefs

- Feedback helps me learn and grow in my role.
- I can choose how I respond when someone offers me feedback.
- While I'm open to considering feedback, I'm also open to rejecting some, all or none of it.
- I am a work in progress.
- Someone has just offered me an opinion from their understanding.
- Feedback is data and information. It is insight.

'It depends'

When I'm running onsite workshops, I'll ask this question:

What do you believe about receiving feedback?

It doesn't take long for someone to respond with, 'Well, it depends...'

Love your 'It depends' criteria. They are your feedback filters and help you decide whether you will take the feedback on board or not.

What are your 'It depends' filters? Here are common examples others have suggested as their 'It depends' filters when it comes to receiving feedback:

- Who is offering it?
- What is it about?
- Are they qualified?
- Do I care?
- Is the feedback actionable?
- Do they have all the information?
- What is their intention?

> **Tip:**
> Don't throw the baby out with the bathwater. You might receive the most poorly-delivered feedback from someone you can't stand, and yet it might also be highly valuable feedback. Look for the gold specks in the rubble!

Thinking styles

Thinking styles, or meta programs,[32] are filtering, inputting and referencing processes—one of which is the way in which we process information, including any feedback offered to us. These thinking styles are learnt and contextual. They are not personality types—think of them as 'habits of thinking' (which means there is room for us to gain flexibility in them).

There are no right or wrong ways to process the feedback offered to you; just useful and less useful ways. The only way thinking styles can go wrong is if a person is 'stuck' at one end of the spectrum of thinking styles, with no flexibility to change their perspective.

Let's take a look at three thinking styles relevant to receiving feedback:

1. internal/external authority
2. counting/discounting
3. matching/mismatching

Internal/external authority

Description: This thinking style is about the place where we look for authority. Some people look internally to their own thoughts and feelings, while others look externally to outside factors. It is about decision making and whether we back our own thoughts and opinions, or not.

Internal authority

I trust myself/my gut/my intuition; I decide for myself/back myself.

People who mostly think at the 'internal' end of the authority spectrum:

- evaluate things based on what they think is appropriate
- make their own decisions, sometimes without the appropriate approval
- motivate themselves
- know what they want, need, believe, feel and value
- might have a closed mind to learning

- dislike tight supervision
- want to decide for themselves
- easily form their own opinions
- may experience conflict with others who also rely on their internal authority
- may ignore what others think
- may ignore feedback.

▶▶ *Reactions*

When it comes to receiving feedback, if the thinking style of the person offered the feedback is positioned more towards the 'internal authority' end of the authority spectrum, a conversation might go like this:

You: 'You are doing a great job on the XYZ project.'

Them: 'No I'm not.' (While thinking: 'You have no idea what kind of job I'm doing.')

Leaders require internal authority at times. It is great for anyone to be confident backing himself/herself when making decisions they know are going to be unpopular or challenged. Internal authority is also useful in the context of receiving feedback from people who do not share the same bigger picture.

Internal authority, when overdone, can get in the way of listening to and considering feedback. A person stuck at the 'internal authority' end of the spectrum's first response to feedback could be thinking: 'Shut up! I know best, and I'm not interested in your feedback.' People who think in this way would usually be positioned towards the bottom of the Feedback Receiving ladder (see page 46, or 119).

External authority

What do you think? . . . It's up to you, what do others think? . . . Let's check the research, I'll Google it . . .

People who mostly think at the 'external authority' end of the authority spectrum:

- evaluate things based on the outside world of rules, people and events
- look outside themselves for guidance, information, motivation and decisions
- feel lost without guidance; may need help to make decisions
- may be people pleasers
- care about what others think
- use information from external sources; and language such as 'authority', 'right', 'wrong', 'proper' and 'acceptable'
- may personalise feedback and use it for feeling bad about themselves
- need feedback from others
- enjoy feedback, validation, praise and affirmation
- can be devastated by 'negative' feedback.

▶▶ *Reactions*

When it comes to receiving feedback, if the thinking style of the person offered the feedback is positioned more towards the 'external authority' end of the authority spectrum, a conversation might go like this:

You: 'You are doing a great job on the XYZ project.'

Them: 'Thanks, that means a lot to me. I've been working really hard on it, so I was hoping you would say that. What a relief, I wasn't sure how I was going. Your feedback is reassuring.'

When it comes to receiving feedback, considering your own opinion as to how you are going can be more valuable when you also add an external check. In other words, back yourself and also check in with someone whose opinion you value. This technique is referred to as 'internal authority with an external check'.

Counting/discounting

Description: This thinking style is related to our ability to value, recognise, acknowledge and celebrate our progress and achievements—but that can also mean being stuck in the opposite mindset of devaluing, diminishing and downplaying our progress and achievements.

Counting

Getting there; making progress; growing; learning; improving; baby steps . . .

People who mostly think at the 'counting' end of the spectrum:
- feel motivated and that they are gaining momentum
- have the ability to see incremental progress over time
- take credit, validate, affirm, recognise, acknowledge, add up the small steps
- reflect on successes, even small ones
- congratulate themselves
- are open to acknowledgement feedback
- value and celebrate acknowledgement feedback offered by others.

▶▶ *Reactions*

When it comes to receiving feedback, if the thinking style of the person offered the feedback is positioned more towards the 'counting' end of the spectrum, a conversation might go like this:

You: 'You are doing a great job on the XYZ project.'

Them: 'Thanks, I've been working really hard on it and have made a lot of progress.'

'Counting' is a thinking style in which the value is seen in what has been achieved and permission is granted by oneself to celebrate. Sometimes we can count and celebrate what others are doing well, but then use negative self-talk about ourselves. We count and celebrate the achievements of others, then discount our own achievements. This keeps us stuck in the mindset of 'it's never enough'. With that mindset, we might receive acknowledgement feedback—and our first response could be to reject it.

Discounting

'Not enough... Not good enough/smart enough/fast enough... Yeah, but it's only...'

People who mostly think at the 'discounting' end of the spectrum:
- think 'I should have done better/more'
- discount the value of what they are doing and learning
- do not take any pleasure in achieving the small steps
- discount small beginnings, which might prevent them from learning through trial and error
- can discount distractions and feedback from others, even when useful
- can have trouble accepting acknowledgement feedback
- may discount feedback from others.

▶▶ *Reactions*

When it comes to receiving feedback, if the thinking style of the person offered the feedback is positioned more towards the 'discounting' end of the spectrum, a conversation might go like this:

You: 'You are doing a great job on the XYZ project.'

Them: 'Not really, I'd like to have been further along than where I am.'

Discounting acknowledgement feedback will also negatively affect motivation. Discounting progress keeps someone stuck at zero. It feels hard for them to gain momentum and build on that zero.

When someone has taken the time to offer acknowledgement feedback, you might like to thank them rather than reject their feedback. We all need to give ourselves permission, (yes, 'permission'—from self to self) to be open to the feedback. The intention of the person offering feedback is probably just to help the other person recognise the progress they are making.

> **Tip:**
> Don't be a feedback rejecter!

Matching/mismatching

Description: This thinking style relates to how we process, filter and compare information. Do we first look for what is the same/similar, or do we first look for what is different?

Matching (sameness)

Same; in common; exactly the same; identical; stable; similar; like; matching; routine...

People who mostly think at the 'matching' end of the spectrum:
- want stability; their security is based on having no changes
- search for commonalities
- search for correlations
- are best at repetitive tasks that do not change
- search for sameness between current experience and previous experience
- value security, regularity, consistency and stability
- do not like change
- thrive on rituals, routine and repetition
- love language like 'mutual agreement', 'security', 'what you both want'

- respond with, 'Isn't this like. . .?'
- may feel insecure if changes are too large or too frequent
- are comfortable doing the same thing over and over
- are calm and stable, not disruptive.

▶▶ *Reactions*

When it comes to receiving feedback, if the thinking style of the person offered the feedback is positioned more towards the 'matching' end of the spectrum, a conversation might go like this:

You: 'You are doing a great job on the XYZ project.'

Them: 'Thanks, I agree, and I'll implement the steps you asked me to today.'

Mismatching (differences)

New; change; different; unique; flip; switch . . .

People who mostly think at the 'mismatching' end of the spectrum:
- first notice things that differ
- want, need and create change
- may force changes that others consider unnecessary
- change the situation if a change to the existing situation does not happen within a certain timeframe
- search for distinctions and exceptions
- value change, variety and newness
- find static situations boring
- will notice differences, problems and things that do not fit
- love terms such as 're-engineering', 'innovation', 'different', 'troubleshooting', 'adventurous', 'evolving' and 'new'
- are best at roles in which projects change every few months
- need variety in tasks within a role
- are happy to change agreements, plans, and goals
- thrive on newness and starting from scratch

- love a blank canvas and revolutionary thinking
- can get bored or restless if there is not enough change for them
- may mismatch feedback offered to them by responding with, 'Yes, but . . .'
- may not implement the feedback offered to them because they know a 'different' way.

▶▶ *Reactions*

When it comes to receiving feedback, if the thinking style of the person offered the feedback is positioned more towards the 'mismatching' end of the spectrum, a conversation might go like this:

You: 'You are doing a great job on the XYZ project.'

Them: 'No I'm not. (Then thinking: 'And don't tell me how to do it.')

The ability to accept and implement feedback requires matching. Being in rapport, building trust and learning, all require matching. Someone who is at the extreme 'mismatching' end of the spectrum has a difficult time receiving and implementing feedback. They have a hard time following instructions.

Taken to the extreme, they will mismatch the feedback conversation process. When asked to meet at 2:00pm, they will suggest 2:30pm (for no reason). They may mismatch the feedback conversation by arguing with the person offering the feedback, changing the subject, and not implementing the feedback once it has been offered to them. They would typically be positioned at the bottom of the Feedback Receiving ladder.

> **Tip:**
> If you are likely to be offering feedback to a person who characteristically 'mismatches', talk about the 'matching' and 'mismatching' thinking styles in the warm-up conversation you have with them. You may even notice them trying to mismatch during your warm-up conversation!

BRINGING IT ALL TOGETHER

Use these mindset improvement strategies for improving feedback receiving skills (your own or those of the people you lead).

1 Quality check the usefulness of personal beliefs about receiving feedback.
2 Use the strategy of 'internal authority with an external check'.
3 Count and celebrate acknowledgement feedback offered, rather than discounting it.
4 Match the feedback before you mismatch.

15
Power

We are more powerful than we might realise when it comes to choosing how we respond to feedback when it is offered. According to Dr L. Michael Hall we have four ways to respond to anything—including feedback.[33]

Our four personal powers

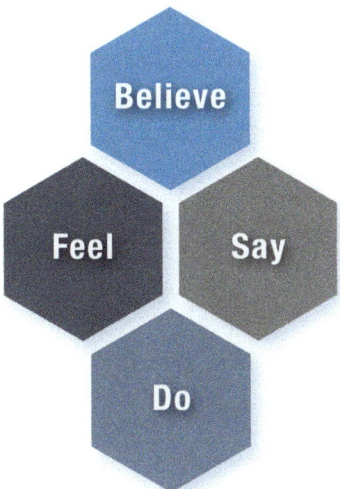

We have:
- the power to choose what we **believe** about the feedback
- the power to choose how we **feel** about the feedback
- the power to choose what we **say** in response to the feedback
- the power to choose what we **do** in response to the feedback.

The power to choose what we BELIEVE

This includes the power to choose what we BELIEVE about feedback that is offered to us.

▶▶ *One person's story: Chloe*

Chloe is a first year PhD candidate. She apprehensively submitted her very first draft of a paper to her supervisor. He returned the document to her with a sea of blue corrections (because he was using 'track changes'). The initial meaning she gave to his feedback was:

> *There is so much blue! He thinks I'm dumb.*

Chloe felt disheartened. So I asked her what else she could make his feedback mean—and she looked puzzled. I asked in another way, which began the following conversation:

Me: 'What's a different way of thinking about his feedback? What's a different spin you could put on it?'

Chloe: 'Maybe I'm just not smart enough to do a PhD. He is disappointed in me.'

Me: 'When you give his feedback those meanings, how do you feel?'

Chloe: 'Stupid, not good enough, worried.'
(These are not useful meanings or feelings!)

Me: 'How else could you think about it?'

I could see that Chloe was on the verge of tears, so I started offering ideas and, together, we brainstormed a list:

- 'He is trying to help me.'
- 'He sees potential in me.'
- 'He wants me to succeed.'
- 'He is setting the expectations for all my future papers.'
- 'He is doing his job.'
- 'He is highly detailed.'
- 'It's the first time I have done this—of course I'm going to get lots of feedback.'

- 'I'm learning.'
- 'I will get better.'
- 'I'm a work in progress.'

As we stepped back to consider all the possible meanings Chloe could give to the feedback, I asked which meaning sat best with her, and explained she had the power to make anything mean anything.

Chloe chose a combination of two: 'He is doing his job and I'm learning.'

Me: 'Now how do you feel?'

Chloe: 'Better.'

Note: Chloe's supervisor had made a number of 'positive' (acknowledgement) comments about her work, but her brain had discounted those and zoomed in on the 'negatives'.

Meaning makers

Have you ever been in a meeting, and someone has made a joke about you? You laugh, but at the same time you are wondering:

Was that a joke, or a dig at me? I'm not sure how to take that comment.

In that moment, you are in the process of deciding what to make the comment mean to you. You are being a meaning maker. You can make anything mean anything!

When someone offers you feedback you could make the feedback mean:

They are trying to help and support me.

You could just as easily make the feedback mean:

They are trying to humiliate and belittle me.

Or you could give it the meaning:

They see me; they see my potential.

Or you could make it mean:

Why are they sucking up to me?

We get to decide what we make feedback mean. We have the power to choose what we believe about any feedback offered to us. We are that powerful!

A key component to being more open to considering feedback is flexibility in our thinking. It's about knowing we have a choice in how we think about the feedback offered to us. It's about our ability to make anything mean anything.

When someone offers us feedback, we make sense of it by processing it through our own beliefs, values and thinking styles, and then attributing meaning to it. This explains why two people can receive exactly the same feedback and one person feels encouraged and supported, while the other feels devastated and disheartened.

What are beliefs?

Our thoughts about anything are just thoughts; we don't give them much meaning, power or energy. We think them into existence and then they disappear, having had little effect on us. They are just brain chatter and we don't *feel* much when we think them. Research has suggested we have 60,000–80,000 thoughts each day.[34] That's a lot of brain chatter!

According to American psychologist, Dr L. Michael Hall, a belief is different from a thought. It is a confirmed thought. It's a thought to which we have each said, 'Yes—that's TRUE for me!' We have decided to change the thought into a belief, but the process of doing that is often outside our conscious awareness.

When you confirm a thought as true for you, you send messages throughout your body via your central nervous system. You embody that thought as a belief. To you, it feels true. You may even say, 'I know it's true. I feel strongly about it.' Your confirmed thoughts become your beliefs, and they make up your belief systems. Your beliefs, in turn, inform your behaviours.

Types of beliefs

It is helpful to categorise beliefs into two broad categories (knowing there will be grey areas). The two categories of beliefs are:

1   limiting beliefs
2   useful beliefs.

Because we each decide what is true for us, we can decide the degree to which we value the feedback offered to us. For example, if your goal is to be more open to feedback, a useful belief is, 'I can choose how I think and feel about the feedback offered to me.' A limiting belief which keeps you from being open to feedback is, 'Feedback makes me feel not good enough.'

Limiting beliefs about feedback:

- hold us back from achieving our goals
- restrict our choices
- disempower us.

Here are some examples of expressions of limiting beliefs about and attitudes to feedback:

- 'I am easily upset by feedback.'
- 'I try to ignore and not worry about negative feedback, but I can't stop thinking about it.'
- 'I always take feedback personally.'

Useful beliefs about feedback:

- help us to achieve our goals
- open up more choices
- empower us.

Here are some examples of expressions of useful beliefs/attitudes in regard to feedback:

- 'I can choose how I feel about feedback offered to me.'
- 'I give myself permission to reject and disregard feedback offered to me.'
- 'I am working on improving my feedback receiving skills.'

Flexibility

Flexibility in our beliefs helps us to receive feedback. It empowers us to have more choice in how we respond to feedback when it is offered to us.

When we consciously choose what we believe about the feedback offered, we feel more in control. For example, if you believe, 'Negative feedback MAKES me feel angry', you are right, because your brain will look for evidence to make that true for you. (We love being right!)

Here is a more useful belief about 'negative' feedback:

> *Negative feedback can't MAKE me feel anything. I CHOOSE to feel angry about the feedback depending upon what I choose to believe about it.*

The power to choose how we FEEL

The power to 'choose how we FEEL' includes the power to choose how we feel about feedback that is offered to us.

Neuroscientist, Dr Lisa Feldman Barrett's theory of constructed emotion[35] is useful in this regard because it is the idea that our feelings come from our beliefs. There are other theories, but I like this one because it gives me more choice—it's empowering. It means that psychologically healthy people are not at the mercy of their emotions and that we are never stuck with an emotion we don't want to feel.

If you make the feedback you receive mean, 'I am not good enough' ...'I am a failure' ... 'What have I done wrong this time?' ... 'I'm going to look stupid' . . .'I've let people down', etc. you may experience a stress response.

If our brains perceive 'negative' feedback as a *danger* to our worth as people or to our reputations, or as a *threat* to who we believe we are, we can feel a range of physical and emotional changes when receiving feedback we consider to be 'negative'.

Physical responses

Physically, we can feel our heart rates increase and an increase of tension in our bodies. Many people feel like the blood rushes from their head, affecting their ability to think—which they describe as 'going blank'. Other people feel a rise in body temperature, reddening of the face, and an increase in perspiration. Please be assured these are normal human responses to perceived danger.

Emotional responses

Emotionally, we may feel a sense of anxiety, fear, or of being overwhelmed, and may experience irritability or restlessness. Our minds might become more focused on the perceived threat, and we may have difficulty concentrating and listening. It is common to have racing thoughts about the 'negative' feedback: 'Am I looking stupid here? . . . Have I stuffed up? . . . Do I need to change? . . . Have I unintentionally hurt someone I care about? . . . Have I finally been exposed as not being as smart as they think I am? . . . Am I going to lose my job?'

How to deal with emotions as responses

When, in response to feedback, you experience an emotion that you consider is not useful, be kind to yourself. Ask for a time-out and give yourself space to deal with your emotions and move through them. If possible, go for a walk (or, at least, get up and move). Ask to 'circle back', if you feel you need to. Ask for time to process the feedback and then get back to the person who offered it so you can ask some clarification questions.

Remember the cool-down conversations? Make use of them. That will allow you time to reflect on your first power (the power to choose what you *believe* about feedback). Ask yourself:

- What am I making this feedback mean that is causing me to feel this way?
- What else could I make it mean?
- What different perspective could I take in regard to this feedback?

If it is impossible for you to leave the meeting, or the room, notice your stress response and whether your armours of self-protection show up. We will explore those armours later in this chapter (see pages 151–5).

Remember, you are human, you experience emotions, and you are always trying to keep yourself safe from real or perceived danger. The trick is to acknowledge the emotions you are feeling and still be present in a professional way. It's okay to experience emotion—it is not okay to express it in a harmful or unprofessional manner.

Following are examples of emotional responses you may have associated with receiving feedback in the past. (The definitions/explanations are based on those in Dr Brené Brown's book *Atlas of the Heart: Mapping meaningful connection and the language of human experience*.[36]) I have adjusted the definitions to make them more relevant to feedback. I do recommend you read the book—it is fabulous!

Stress

Stress is emotional strain resulting from demanding or adverse circumstances. We can feel this way if we evaluate feedback we have received as something with which we are unable to cope successfully. This is more likely when the feedback was not predictable, feels out of our control or we feel overloaded.

Anxiety

We may experience anxiety as an emotional response characterised by feelings of tension, worried thoughts and physical changes, like increased blood pressure. When we receive feedback, there are times we may feel like we are losing control of the situation and could begin worst-case scenario thinking, leading to anxiety.

Worry

Worry is the feeling associated with concern over actual or potential problems. We might worry after receiving some kinds of feedback, meaning our thinking extends into the future.

Dread

Dread causes us to anticipate the future with great apprehension or fear. It occurs frequently in response to high probability negative events. If we make feedback conversations into 'high probability negative events', it makes sense that we may dread them! (This is usually a sign there has been an insufficient warm-up conversation.)

Fear

Fear is a negative, short-lasting, high-alert emotional response to a perceived threat. If we perceive feedback as a threat, it makes sense that we feel fearful. A useful strategy is to identify what it is specifically about the feedback that we perceive as a threat.

Shame

Shame is a feeling of distress caused by consciousness of one's own wrong behaviour. Sometimes people receive feedback on their performance and make it about themselves as a person, rather than just about their actions/behaviour or results. When we do that, we can feel shame, which is a self-evaluating emotion leading to us believing 'I am bad'. The focus is on the self, not the behaviour about which the feedback is received. Dr Brené Brown indicates that shame does not lead to change.[37]

Guilt

Guilt is the discomfort we feel when we evaluate that what we've done, or failed to do, is against our values. It is the emotional response we feel when we receive feedback that we have done something we know to be bad. The focus of the feedback is on the behaviour. Guilt can drive positive change in behaviour.

Embarrassment

Embarrassment is the emotional response we feel when we receive feedback that we have done something observable that makes us feel uncomfortable, but we also know that we are fallible, human and not alone. Embarrassment is short lived and, sometimes, can be funny. It can be a fleeting feeling of self-conscious discomfort in response to feedback that may have minor significance.

Defensiveness

Defensiveness is an impulsive and reactive response employing denial or deflection. It is the way we try to protect our ego and fragile self-esteem. It typically occurs if we personalise the feedback received—making it about the person, not about the performance.

Anger

Anger is an emotional response of annoyance, displeasure or hostility we feel when we believe the feedback offered to us is unjust or gets in the way of our desired outcome. Choosing to stay angry about feedback we have received in the past can make us exhausted and sick. Internalising anger will damage our workplace relationship with the person who offered us the feedback.

How do you want to feel when receiving feedback?

In my Feedback Fitness workshops, I offer everyone in the room a set of cards with fifty different emotions written on them. I then ask them to select their top five cards, in order, to show how they want to feel when receiving feedback.

Following are examples of the common responses. (The definitions/explanations are based on those in Dr Brené Brown's book, *Atlas of the heart: Mapping meaningful connection and the language of human experience*.[38] I have applied the context of feedback.)

Excitement

Excitement is as an energised state of enthusiasm. It can be experienced when we receive useful feedback.

Curiosity

Curiosity arises from recognising a gap in our knowledge about something that interests us and becoming emotionally and cognitively invested in closing that gap. Useful feedback can assist in closing the gap.

Connection

Connection is the energy that exists between people when they feel seen, heard, and valued. It is a feature of the most useful feedback conversations.

Joy

Joy is an intense feeling of pleasure and appreciation. It can be experienced when we receive useful feedback.

Happiness

Happiness is a state of wellbeing, joy and pleasure. It is often associated with immediate feedback offered to us.

Calm

Calm is the absence of strong emotions and allows us to modify our perspective and practise mindfulness. Remaining calm helps us to manage our emotional reactivity when receiving feedback.

Gratitude

Gratitude is an emotional response that reflects deep appreciation. We can feel gratitude for the useful feedback we receive.

Relief

Relief is a feeling of reassurance and relaxation following release from anxiety or distress. Feelings of tension leave the body and we are able to breathe more easily. It is characterised by thoughts of the worst being over and of being safe for the moment. This can often be the emotion felt once feedback has been received and was better than expected.

Pride

Pride is a feeling of pleasure or satisfaction in one's own achievements. This is an emotion we feel when we receive feedback praising our accomplishments or efforts.

Humility

Humility is the feeling of being humble and not thinking we are better than other people. It makes us open to accepting feedback and learning, combined with a balanced and accurate assessment of our own contributions, including our strengths, imperfections and opportunities for growth.

> **Tip:**
> Someone who is feedback resilient knows feedback can't *make* them feel anything. They know they have choice in what they make the feedback mean and, therefore, choice in how they feel about that feedback.

The power to choose what we SAY

The power to 'choose what we SAY' includes the choice of what we say in response to feedback offered to us.

Have you ever been feedback-bombed? This is when you are presented with unexpected feedback—with no warm-up and no cool-down; just feedback you were not expecting, thrown at you out of the blue. In that moment, you might feel shocked. So, it's useful to have a default response ready for times when you could be feedback-bombed.

One immediate response you might to try is: 'Thanks, I might consider that' (whether you might or you might not and, even if you do consider the feedback, you might or might not implement some, all, or any of it). It's a polite and professional response which gives you time to consider the feedback later, if you want to, without the pressure of having to respond in the moment.

Another 'go to' response you can have ready to use, is to ask for clarification: 'Sorry, can you please explain what you mean?' or 'Tell me more' (with genuine curiosity). These questions show the other person you are open to considering their feedback, and you are respectfully trying to understand what is meant by the feedback.

You have the power to choose what you say in response to someone offering you feedback. No one can make you move your mouth and force words out. In response to feedback, you have the power to choose what you say, what you don't say, when you say it, and how you say it.

The power to choose what we DO

The power to 'choose what we DO' includes the choice of what we do in response to feedback offered to us.

Hopefully by now you are feeling empowered to choose how you respond to feedback offered to you: the power to choose what you believe about the feedback (the meaning you give it); the power to choose how you feel about it; the power to choose what you say in response; and now, finally, the power to choose what you do or don't do in response to it.

You are the boss of you. No one can make you do something you don't want to do. There may be consequences of not implementing the feedback offered to you, but there is always choice. Depending on the situation, you have the power to move away from feedback, or the power to lean into it. You also have the power to lean in, and then walk away!

> **Tip:**
> Give yourself permission to reject feedback after you have considered it.

▶▶ *My story: When I gave myself permission to reject feedback*

> I once delivered a leadership workshop and at the end of the day, handed participants paper evaluations to complete. One participant offered me feedback:
>
> > *These evaluations should be online to save time. I don't want to write feedback now; I want time to reflect. It would be much quicker for you to collate the information electronically. Why don't you just use Survey Monkey?'*
>
> I'm sure he meant well.

I could have explained to him that I have experimented with asking participants to complete online evaluations after workshops. I could have explained that, on average, the response rate was only 5% (yes—even with three follow-up emails asking people to complete the survey). I could have explained I stopped trying that approach, because the response rate is 95% when I ask participants to use paper and pen at the end of a workshop given face-to-face.

But I didn't. I politely said, 'Thanks for that', and kept collecting the handwritten evaluations.

What Seth Godin says

In addition to launching one of the most popular blogs in the world,[39] Seth Godin, entrepreneur and speaker, has written twenty-one best-selling books, including: *The dip: A little book that teaches you when to quit (and when to stick)*;[40] *Linchpin: Are you indispensable?*;[41] *Purple cow: Transform your business by being remarkable*;[42] *Tribes: We need you to lead us*;[43] and *What to do when It's your turn (and it's always your turn)*.[44] His book, *This is marketing: You can't be seen until you learn to see*,[45] is acclaimed as having been an instant bestseller in countries around the world.

In his blog, Godin offers the following three reasons why we might **reject** feedback that is offered to us:[46]

1 The person offering feedback is not very good at offering useful feedback.
2 The product, service or performance was not created by us to please the person offering the feedback. That person is not the customer.
3 We're not going to revise what was done any time soon. The 'movie' is made, and specific feedback isn't going to 'get the movie remade'.

He further explains:

Just because criticism is on offer doesn't mean you have to seek it out or even listen to it.

The armour of self-protection

> [Using armor is a way] *in which we self-protect when we feel backed into a corner, when we feel afraid, when we feel anxious, nervous, out of depth, what do we do to self-protect... The greatest barrier to being brave is the armor we throw up when we are feeling less than.*[47]
>
> *Armoring up and protecting our egos rarely leads to productive, kind, and respectful conversations.*[48]
>
> **Dr Brené Brown**

My theory is it's rarely feedback that we avoid, it's the emotions resulting from the feedback. We use armour to try to protect ourselves from feeling those emotions, and it's that armour we see show up as behaviours during our feedback conversations.

We try to keep ourselves safe from emotions we don't want to feel.

Let's take a look at some examples of self-protection armours that can appear when we are offered feedback (especially if there has been no warm-up and we have the limiting belief that receiving feedback is dangerous).

Armour 1: Using perfectionism to try to avoid being offered feedback

> *Perfectionism is not the same as striving for excellence. Perfectionism is not about healthy achievement and growth. Perfectionism is a defensive move... Perfectionism is a twenty-ton shield that we lug around, thinking it will protect us, when in fact it's the thing that's really preventing us from being seen.*
>
> *Perfectionism is not self-improvement. Perfectionism is, at its core, about trying to earn approval. Most perfectionists grew up being praised for achievement and performance... Somewhere along the way, they adopted this dangerous and debilitating belief system: 'I am what I accomplish and how well I accomplish it. Please. Perform. Perfect.' Healthy striving is self-focused: How can I improve? Perfectionism is other-focused: What will they think? Perfectionism is a hustle.*
>
> **Dr Brené Brown**[49]

Ouch! As a recovering perfectionist, Brené Brown's words hit me hard. When we apply perfectionism to receiving feedback, it is easy to see how the fear of failure, of making mistakes, of not meeting other people's expectations, and being seen as 'less than perfect' plays out. It makes sense that a perfectionist would try to avoid feedback conversations.

> *If I look perfect and do everything perfectly, I can avoid or minimize the painful feelings of shame, judgment and blame.*
> **Dr Brené Brown**[50]

Armour 2: Responding with sarcasm

Sarcasm, in the form of banter, is common among members of some teams:

> *We have a great team. We hang sh*t on each other all the time.*

But sarcasm can often take the form of hurtful and passive aggressive comments, and be used to shut down a feedback conversation. The word 'sarcasm' is derived from the Greek for 'flesh', with its literal meaning being interpreted as 'tear the flesh like dogs' (which relates to the way it can be used aggressively). Often rising out of fear and anxiety, sarcasm is an armour that can be used to avoid a feedback conversation. It is a means of rejecting the feedback being offered by cutting off the conversation with a blade so sharp it could 'tear the flesh' of the person offering it.

If you hear yourself using sarcasm in response to feedback, be kind to yourself (and apologise to the other person). The use of sarcasm is a sign you may be feeling threatened, or angry, or that you are 'not enough'. Determine what meaning you are giving the feedback you are offered that is causing you to experience those emotional responses and use the powers you have to choose what you **believe** and how you **feel** about the feedback so you are able to come up with a different, more useful and empowering meaning.

Armour 3: Becoming defensive

Defensiveness in response to being offered feedback comes in many different forms. We can attempt to protect ourselves by blaming others; making excuses; resorting to sarcasm; and challenging the feedback. While it can sound like nothing more than justifications and excuses, there are usually changes in our bodies when we become defensive. Body temperature may rise, and the sound of the voice can change. We might hear ourselves saying: 'Yes, but . . .'; 'It's not my fault . . .'; or 'Nobody told me . . .'

If you notice that your first response when offered feedback is to challenge it, argue or provide evidence to defend yourself, that could be a sign you are feeling threatened by the feedback. The challenge, in the moment, is to have the self-awareness to ask for more details. Give yourself a chance to gather more information—professionally and respectfully asking questions to gain more understanding.

Once you have a greater understanding of the feedback being offered to you, you might like to ask for a break, or ask to come back to the conversation later. Give yourself the time to reflect on what has been offered. Cool-down conversations are super useful at times like this and, sometimes, it might be you—the person to whom the feedback was offered—who leads the cool-down process.

Armour 4: Avoidance

When working with individuals and teams for whom the level of Feedback Fitness is low, I have observed three different types of avoidance. The following three avoidance behaviours usually appear in relation to the offering of **evaluation** feedback during the **workout**, when there is more likelihood of discomfort and emotional response.

1   Avoidance of feedback conversations.
2   Avoidance during feedback conversations.
3   Avoidance after the feedback conversations.

Avoidance of feedback conversations

The following are examples of what might be observed when feedback conversations are being avoided.

- ▶ A culture of 'nice and polite' conversations, rather than conversations which get to the heart of the issues.

- In some instances (but certainly not always), restructures, secondments, and redundancies.
- Undesirable behaviours being tolerated instead of addressed.
- Feedback conversations being repeatedly postponed.
- The intended recipient of the feedback 'accidentally' getting the day, time or location of the meeting wrong.
- The intended recipient of the feedback calling in sick on the day of the scheduled feedback conversation.

Avoidance during feedback conversations

The following are examples of avoidance behaviours that might be evident from both participants during feedback conversations.

- At the last minute, other 'urgent' topics being raised and prioritised over feedback, resulting in the feedback being postponed until the next meeting.
- The recipient of the feedback 'mismatching' in regard to the duration of the meeting: 'I'm sorry I only have ten minutes. I need to leave early.'
- Vague or general feedback being offered, with the person receiving it left to guess what the conversation was about.
- Silence or one-word answers in response to the feedback.
- Changing the subject or answering with defensive questions.
- Becoming aggressive or defensive, blaming others, or making excuses.
- If the conversation is face-to-face, the recipient of the feedback walking out of the room or the building.
- If the conversation is online, the recipient of the feedback having internet issues and 'dropping out' of the meeting.

Avoidance after feedback conversations

The following are examples of avoidance behaviours that might be evident from both participants after feedback conversations.

- Both people avoiding each other.
- The recipient of the feedback avoiding the person who offered the feedback.

- Not offering cool-down conversations.
- Not responding to invitations to take part in cool-down conversations.
- Not responding to phone calls, emails, or messages.
- Taking an unplanned day off work after the feedback conversation.
- Asking to be seconded to a different department.
- Resigning.

16
Confidence and Esteem

An overview

Have you ever started to doubt yourself after receiving feedback (most likely evaluation feedback or guidance feedback)? Do you tend to take feedback personally? I'm going to share with you a more useful way to think about esteem, particularly self-esteem. When you believe feedback cannot influence your self-esteem, you will be more open to receiving it.

On the following pages are six strategies to empower you with more choice in how you respond to feedback when it is offered.

Strategy 1: Consider confidence and esteem as two different things

When it comes to receiving feedback, it is useful to separate 'confidence' from 'esteem'.[51]

'Esteem' is a word meaning 'respect' and 'admiration'. We can hold others in esteem, but self-esteem refers to valuing and respecting ourselves and considering ourselves as worthy of love and belonging.

We will come back to esteem later in this chapter but, first, let's clarify what 'confidence' is, how it differs from 'esteem' and how it is linked to feedback.

Confidence

Confidence is different from esteem. It is usually experienced as a feeling we have about our ability to do something, or to perform a task or skill. For example:

▶ how confident do you feel in your ability to lead a team, write a report, or perform your role?

▶ how confident are you in your ability to tie your shoelace?

When someone asks you how confident you are, ask yourself and/or them, 'Confident in my ability to do what?' Asking this question is a reminder to link confidence to a task or skill.

Since most people experience confidence as a feeling, a great strategy is to rate your level of confidence out of ten. How confident out of ten do feel about your ability to perform a particular task or skill?

An easy example to which most people can relate is the level of confidence we have in our ability to drive a car. Sitting behind the wheel of the car for the first time, many of us probably didn't feel very confident in our ability to drive. We might have rated that confidence level as just one or two out of ten.

The more we practised, the more confident in our driving ability we became. When we felt a high level of confidence in our driving skills (for example eight, nine or ten out of ten), we would have booked in for a driving test.

Passing the test, might have made us feel **really** confident—in fact, overly confident! It might have been false confidence and have not been based on our real skills and driving experience.

If we had failed the test, our confidence in our ability might have dropped to two or three out of ten. But, given the chance for further practice, to ask for more help and to be open to feedback, we could build our confidence in our ability to drive back up, until we felt confident enough to take the test again (and, hopefully, pass).

> **Tip:**
> Confidence is always about your ability to do something.

Strategy 2: Confidence is contextual

People who learn to drive and who earn their licence in small rural towns, might feel highly confident in their ability to drive across town. But, in contrast, they might feel less confident about driving in peak hour traffic in their closest capital city. However if they moved to the city and drove in peak hour traffic every day for two years, their confidence in their ability to drive in the city would increase. You get the idea!

Confidence is contextual. How confident you feel in your ability to do something goes up and down and can be influenced by context.

> **Tip:**
> You can feel very confident in your ability to perform a task in one context, and less confident about your ability in a different context.

Receiving feedback can definitely impact how confident we might feel about our ability to perform a task. At times, feedback can feel like a real boost to confidence and can be a confirmation of personal progress.

At other times, we might allow feedback to decrease our confidence in our ability to do something. Confidence levels go up and down. The great thing about confidence is we can build it back up again over time if we give ourselves the opportunity to practise, are open to feedback and take action to improve.

> **Tip:**
> Confidence is a feeling about your ability to do something. You can rate that feeling (perhaps out of ten). That rating level can go up and down—and that's okay. If your confidence is at a low level, you can use feedback to build it back up.

Strategy 3: 'Esteem' is a *vurrrrb* [verb]!

Now let's turn our attention to 'esteem', and 'self-esteem' in particular.

Self-esteem is different from confidence. Self-esteem is how you *choose* to value yourself and to consider yourself as worthy of love and belonging.

I first learnt about a different way of thinking about self-esteem in an eight-day training course with American psychologist, Dr L. Michael

Hall. It was a challenge for me to change the way I thought about esteem and self-esteem. I kept putting up my hand and asking him clarification questions. Nine times out of ten, his response to my question was, 'Because, Sue, it's a *vurrrrb*' (insert strong American accent here).

If I was ever struggling with my new way of thinking about esteem after I came home from that training, I'd remind myself (also in a thick American accent): 'Because Sue, it's a *vurrrrb*.'

Verbs are doing words, but the more common way of thinking about 'esteem' and 'self-esteem' are as nouns which are naming words. Nouns are the names of things.

If you look for 'esteem' in a dictionary, you will see it is defined as both a noun *and a verb*, depending on the context in which it is used and how it is used. In my opinion, it is a game changer to use 'esteem' contextually as a verb—a doing word. When you think about 'esteem' as a noun, you make it a thing, which is not as useful as thinking of it as something you can do. That way of interpreting the word is the game changer!

> **Tip:**
> Consider esteem as something you do; a verb. In that way, you are able to take the action to esteem yourself.

Have you ever heard people talking about someone having 'low self-esteem' and that they needed 'higher self-esteem'? That is typically the end of the conversation, without much discussion of how a person could 'raise' their self-esteem or prevent it from decreasing. One message sent to many of us from our childhood days was to: 'Find something you are good at, and be the best at it that you can be—that way you can feel good about yourself.' (This is not useful!)

When 'esteem' is considered as a verb, rather than a noun, it makes sense that it cannot be assessed in highs or lows. Any feedback you choose to perceive as 'negative', can't lower, take away or diminish the manner in which you esteem yourself, because that is an action towards yourself over which you alone have control.

> **Tip:**
> Considering self-esteem as a verb puts **you** in charge, because it is an action you alone do.

If you have been considering 'esteem' as a noun, thinking if it as a doing word instead may take a bit of getting used to. Be open to this.

It may help if you find the things you will be 'doing' when you think about esteem as a verb. Examples of that include:

- you will be decid**ing** you are valuable and worthwhile just because you exist in the world
- you will be valu**ing** yourself
- you will be choos**ing** to value yourself
- you will be consider**ing** yourself as valuable, and worthy of love and belonging.

In other words, you will be esteem**ing** yourself!

> **Tip:**
> Get busy esteeming yourself!

Strategy 4: Feedback is about performance/behaviour, not your worth as a person

If you think about 'esteem' as a verb, you decide that your worth as a person is a given—you don't need to earn it by 'being good at something'. You can decide that your worth as a person is inherent and was granted to you at birth. No one holds a newborn baby and asks whether that baby is worthy and valuable: 'Welcome to the world little one! Now, what are you good at? Have you won any awards? I can only value you based on your achievements . . .'

The acceptance of the worth of the newborn child goes without saying.

Take the approach that is taken towards a newborn baby and apply it to yourself. You can decide to value yourself for no other reason than you are human, you are here and you exist. You don't need to 'earn' your worth through your achievements. Your failures (and you will fail, because you are human) cannot 'decrease' your worth as a human. You are not your failures, and neither are you your achievements. There is a valuable and worthy essence of you and, separate to that, there are all the things you do in the world. You are more than those things.

Approaching 'esteem' as a verb takes all the pressure off trying to establish your value and sense of worth as a result of your work and work-related feedback—especially acknowledgement feedback. It takes away the need to rely on feedback for feeling good about yourself.

> **Tip:**
> If you have linked your worth as a person to your performance, 'negative' feedback may feel like a personal attack!

Think of feedback as information and data about your behaviour, actions, decisions, skills, planning ability, lack of planning ability, etc. and not about you as a person. At times, your performance may be bad, but you are not bad—and 'negative' feedback doesn't make you bad. You might make a terrible decision at work, but that does not make you a terrible person.

> *I might say, 'That shot sucked,' but I tried not to tell myself that I sucked.*
>
> Karrie Webb (one of Australia's greatest golfers)[52]

Strategy 5: Flat line esteem—esteem does not go up and down

Suppose someone offers you feedback on the way you formatted a particular report.

Thank the person who offered the feedback for their feedback, despite your confidence in your ability to format that report (and future reports like it) having been reduced as a result of their feedback. Remember, using your four powers of choice, you are able to choose how you respond by deciding what you make any feedback offered to you mean, and you are able to ask further questions about specific changes and improvements you can make in the future.

In other words, the changes you can make to the way you format that report moving forward are within your control. You can ask for guidance feedback and you are able to build your confidence in your formatting skills.

If you are thinking about esteem as a noun, you will be linking your worth as a person to your performance. Receiving feedback on the report you submitted will decrease your confidence in your formatting skills and will decrease **your self-esteem**. You will feel bad about the 'mistakes' you made in the report, and you will feel bad about **yourself**. This is not useful.

The more useful way to think about feedback is that it may change your *confidence* in your ability to perform a skill. That change can be in both directions—an increase in confidence or a decrease in confidence. When you are offered acknowledgement feedback (like 'You are doing a great job'), your confidence in performing the skill involved might increase. When you are offered evaluation feedback (like 'Your performance is not meeting expectations'), your confidence in performing that skill might decrease—but that's okay!

While your confidence levels can go up and down, your esteem remains unaffected (remember, 'esteem' is a vurrrrb)!

> **Tip:**
> Your confidence in your ability to perform a skill may go up and down, but the decision to value yourself and, therefore, the action of esteeming yourself, remains a flat, unwavering line.

Strategy 6: Feedback is useful, but you don't *need* it to feel good about yourself

Choose to be the best you can be in your position at work, or in your passion outside of work, because you *want* to—not because you *need* to do it to feel good about yourself.

If you ask for feedback:

▶ ask for acknowledgement feedback to stay motivated

- ask for evaluation feedback to find out how you are going according to expectations
- ask for guidance feedback to improve your performance in the future.

Don't ask for feedback to validate you as a human being, or to make you feel good about yourself. It is risky and disempowering to try to gain a sense of value as a person through feedback from others that is based on your behaviour and performance. Putting your own sense of worth into someone else's hands doesn't work (I've tried it!). Even if you do get 'acknowledgement feedback', your sense of worth as a person will only last until the next task presents itself and the feedback related to that task is offered. That means every task is a threat to your worth as a person—how exhausting! Get off that esteem rollercoaster!

> **Tip:**
> Ask for feedback to strive for excellence in a healthy, continuous improvement kind of way. Don't rely on 'positive' feedback to feel good about yourself or allow 'negative' feedback to 'make you feel bad about yourself'. That is disempowered thinking—and you deserve better than that!

17
Conclusion

BRINGING IT ALL TOGETHER

Play lightly

You may have noticed by now that the topic of feedback is a complex one. It is hoped that enough information has been covered in this book to enable you to build solid ground on which to stand for your future feedback conversations. Your confidence and courage in feedback conversations will continue to increase the more you give yourself a chance to try the strategies introduced here. Take your time. Be kind to yourself. Baby steps are worth celebrating, so celebrate incremental progress over time!

Please do keep in mind that not everyone in your team or your family will be 'Feedback Fit'. Be gentle with them. Hopefully, when you realise someone's armour has appeared during a feedback conversation, you will respond with kindness and compassion. Now you know how to choose how you respond when someone offers you poorly-delivered feedback. You can sift through the rubble to find the specks of gold.

Use it or lose it

Having a framework for your future feedback conversations is empowering—and it's even more empowering to implement that framework. Are you committed to implementing strategies to transform the way you offer and receive feedback? The three steps of the Feedback Fitness framework (the warm-up, the workout and the cool-down) are similar to the legs in a triathlon; you will perform best when you practise all three steps. Choose your least favourite of the three and take action to make that your superpower.

Back yourself

You have expertise and experience in leading your team. You are the one who knows yourself and the members of your team best. Take the framework described in this book and make it work for your leadership style and your team members. Apply your own way of saying things. Trust your instincts. Back yourself.

You've got this!

Endnotes

1. Zavvy (Deel Engage), 11 January 2024, *46 employee engagement statistics HR managers should know,* viewed 8 February 2024, <https://www.zavvy.io/blog/employee-engagement-statistics>.

2. Zavvy (Deel Engage), 9 January 2024, *Employee retention strategy 101 (+ expert tips from L&D professionals),* viewed 8 February 2024, <https://www.zavvy.io/blog/employee-retention-strategy>.

3. Zavvy (Deel Engage), 11 January 2024, op. cit. (citing the *New York Times*).

4. Ibid. (citing the *Harvard Business Review*).

5. Perry, E. August 2023, *5 generations in the workplace: How to manage them all,* BetterUp, 2024, viewed 8 February 2024, <https://www.betterup.com/blog/generations-in-the-workplace>.

6. Owl Labs, 2023, *State of hybrid work, remote work, office work 2022,* viewed 8 February 2024, <https://resources.owllabs.com/state-of-remote-work>.

7. Zavvy (Deel Engage), 11 January 2024, op. cit.

8. Folkman, J., June 2015, '*The best way to deliver tough feedback: Stop talking and start listening*', Forbes Media L.L.C. 2024, viewed 8 February 2024, <https://www.forbes.com/sites/joefolkman/2015/06/25/the-best-way-to-deliver-tough-feedback-stop-talking-and-start-listening/?sh=70e0bf2864fb>.

9. Zenger, J. and Folkman, J., 30 April 2015, 'The assumptions that make giving tough feedback even tougher', Harvard Business Publishing, 2024, viewed 8 February 2024, <https://hbr.org/2015/04/the-assumptions-that-make-giving-tough-feedback-even-tougher>.

10. Safe Work Australia, 2019, *Work-related psychological health and safety: A systematic approach to meeting your duties,* pdf, viewed 8 February 2024, <https://www.safeworkaustralia.gov.au/system/files/documents/1911/work-related_psychological_health_and_safety_a_systematic_approach_to_meeting_your_duties.pdf>

11. Edmondson, Professor A. C., 2020, *Psychological safety: Clear blocks to innovation, collaboration, and risk-taking,* LinkedIn course, viewed 13 April 2024, <https://www.linkedin.com/learning/psychological-safety-clear-blocks-to-innovation-collaboration-and-risk-taking/psychological-safety-clear-blocks-to-problem-solving-and-innovation>

12. Brook, Dr L., 5 January 2024, author's Zoom interview.
13. Sinek, S. 2023, LinkedIn, viewed 9 February 2024, <https://www.linkedin.com/posts/simonsinek_some-of-the-human-skills-that-are-underappreciated-activity-7029842923072450561-lg-x/>
14. Routh, Z., 3 November 2023, author's Zoom interview.
15. Brown, B., 2021(a), *The dare to lead glossary: Key language, skills, tools, and practices*, Brené Brown LLC, Houston, TX, p. 4.
16. Brown, B., 2021(b), *The dare to lead read-along workbook*, Brené Brown LLC, Houston, TX, p. 11.
17. Grant, Dr A., 2021, 'Persuading the Unpersuadable', *Harvard Business Review*, March–April 2021.
18. Heath, D., 2020, *Upstream: The quest to solve problems before they happen*, Avid Reader Press/Simon & Schuster, New York, NY.
19. Brook, Dr L., 5 January 2024, author's Zoom interview.
20. Brown, B. and Guillen, B. (host), 27 September 2022, *The hardest feedback I've ever received: Part 2*, (podcast, transcript), viewed 10 February 2024, <https://brenebrown.com/podcast/the-hardest-feedback-ive-ever-received-part-2-of-2/#transcript>.
21. Dr Kristin Neff is a pioneer in the field of self-compassion (or the practice of 'turning compassion inward') and has written several books on the subject.
22. Solomon, L., 9 March 2019, 'Two-thirds of managers are uncomfortable communicating with employees', *Harvard Business Review*, March 2019.
23. Chapman, Dr G., 2024, 'What are the five love languages?', *Love languages*, viewed 11 February 2024, <https://5lovelanguages.com/learn>.
24. Brown, B., 2021(c), *Atlas of the heart: Mapping meaningful connection and the language of human experience*, Random House, New York, NY.
25. Dweck, C. S., 2006, *Mindset: The new psychology of success*, Random House, New York, NY.
26. Brown, B., 2021(a), op. cit.
27. Brook, Dr L., 5 January 2024, author's Zoom interview.
28. Brown, B., 2018, *Dare to lead: Brave work. Tough conversations. Whole hearts*, Random House, New York, NY, p. 49.
29. Brown, B. and Guillen, B. (host), 27 September 2022, op. cit.
30. Brown, B., 2018, op.cit., p. 203.

31 Hall, Dr L. M., 2000, *Secrets of personal mastery: Advanced techniques for accessing your higher levels of consciousness*, Crown House Publishing, Carmarthen, p. 64.

32 Meta programs are neuro-linguistic program filters or mental processes that shape how we perceive, process, and respond to information. Richard Bandler introduced the idea of meta programs to neuro-linguistic programming in the late 1970s. Leslie Cameron-Bandler and others investigated further, using the Meta Model to identify a list of meta program patterns for use in therapy.

33 Hall, Dr L. M., 2000, op. cit.

34 Shahmoradian, Dr F. S., 2020, *Mental metamorphism*, Authorhouse, Bloomington, Indiana, IN.

35 Barrett, L. F., 2017, 'The theory of constructed emotion: An active inference account of interoception and categorization', *Social Cognitive and Affective Neuroscience*, vol. 12, no. 1, January 2017, pp. 1–23.

36 Brown, B., 2021(c), op. cit.

37 Ibid.

38 Brown, B., 2021(c), op. cit.

39 Godin, S., nd, *Seth's Site*, viewed 19 February 2024, <https://www.sethgodin.com>.

40 Godin, S., 2007, *The dip: A little book that teaches you when to quit (and when to stick)*, Portfolio (Penguin/Random House), New York, NY.

41 Godin, S., 2010, *Linchpin: Are you indispensable?*, Portfolio (Penguin/Random House), New York, NY.

42 Godin, S., 2004, *Purple cow: Transform your business by being remarkable*, Michael Joseph, London.

43 Godin, S., 2011, *Tribes: We need you to lead us*, Piatkus Books, London.

44 Godin, S., 2014, *What to do when It's your turn (and it's always your turn)*, The Domino Project, New York, NY.

45 Godin, S., 2018, *This is marketing: You can't be seen until you learn to see*, Penguin, New York, NY.

46 Godin, S., 1 July 2023, 'Actionable feedback', *Seth's Blog*, viewed 19 February 2024, <https://seths.blog/2023/07/actionable-feedback>

47 Brown, B. (host), 5 April 2021, 'Brené on armored versus daring leadership', Part 1 of 2, (podcast transcript), *Dare to lead with Brené Brown*, Parcast Network, accessed 20 February 2024, <https://brenebrown.com/podcast/brene-on-armored-versus-daring-leadership-part-1-of-2>.

48 Brown, B., 15 October 2018, 'Clear Is Kind. Unclear Is Unkind.', *Brené Brown*, (blog), viewed 10 February 2024, <https://brenebrown.com/articles/2018/10/15/clear-is-kind-unclear-is-unkind>.

49 Brown, B., *Daring greatly: How the courage to be vulnerable transforms the way we live, love, parent, and lead*, Gotham Books (Penguin), New York, NY, Chapter 4.

50 Brown, B., 2021(a), op.cit., p. 12.

51 The distinction between 'self-esteem' and 'self-confidence' is explained in detail on page 87 of Dr L. Michael Hall's, *The crucible: And the fires of change*, published in 2010 by the *International Society of Neuro-Semantics®*, Clifton, Colorado.

52 Webb, K, nd, *The Howie Games* (podcast by Mark Howard), Apple Podcasts, viewed 16 April 2024, <https://podcasts.apple.com/gb/podcast/84-karrie-webb-pt-b/id1146329262?i=1000466068562>

Work with Sue

With over sixteen years of working with leaders, Sue Anderson has created the Feedback Fitness framework to build the skills and confidence of those with whom she works. She is a speaker, trainer, facilitator and leadership coach who loves to help leaders create safe and empowered spaces from which to operate.

Essentially, Sue is a communication and empowerment expert for leaders. She is renowned for her use of powerful questions, delivered at just the right time to challenge thinking and unveil blind spots.

Sue's clients include CEOs, directors, managers, coordinators and team leaders across a wide variety of industries. She has worked with corporate organisations, professional service practices, not-for-profit organisations, and government (at both local and state level).

Sue writes a weekly blog and shares her thoughts via her newsletter, which you can subscribe to at: www.sue-anderson.com.au

To find out more about Sue's workshops, her speaking availability and her coaching programs, visit: www.sue-anderson.com.au

Contact Sue by email, at: sue@sue-anderson.com.au

Or by phone, on: 0417 052 739

Scan below to sign up for Sue's weekly newsletter. You can unsubscribe at any time.

By the same author

Available from:
https://www.sue-anderson.com.au/products/unshakeable-at-work

Available from:
https://www.sue-anderson.com.au/products/unbullyable

www.ingramcontent.com/pod-product-compliance
Lightning Source LLC
Chambersburg PA
CBHW040551010526